Young People's Literature in Series: Fiction

Young People's Literature in Series: Fiction

An Annotated Bibliographical Guide

JUDITH K. ROSENBERG
&
KENYON C. ROSENBERG

1972

Libraries Unlimited, Inc.

Littleton, Colo.

Copyright © 1972 Judith K. Rosenberg and Kenyon C. Rosenberg
All Rights Reserved
Printed in the United States of America

Library of Congress Card Number 72-93401
International Standard Book Number 0-87287-060-X

LIBRARIES UNLIMITED, INC.
P.O. Box 263
Littleton, Colorado 80120

Z1037
R69

TABLE OF CONTENTS

Introduction 7

Fiction Series 9

Series Title Index 153

Title Index 159

DEDICATION

To young people's librarians
and
to those young people.

INTRODUCTION

This bibliography is intended to be a book selection tool (through the evaluative annotations) and an aid to guiding the reading of young people. It is divided into two main sections: 1) fiction series and 2) non-fiction series. This first volume contains the fiction series, while the forthcoming volume will deal with publishers' and non-fiction series.

Among the fiction series listed herein are both those in print and those out of print. The year 1955 was chosen as the earliest imprint date acceptable, since Frank Gardner's *Sequels* (London, Library Association, Association of Assistant Librarians, 1955) covers most series up to this date. The only exceptions are older series with new title additions after 1955.

Because of their transitory nature, series titles aimed at the kindergarten through grade 2 reader have been omitted. However, some series whose subjects might appeal to older reluctant readers with a grade 2 reading level have been included. The over-all level of the series found here is for grades 3 through 9. Several adult titles that might be enjoyed by young people have been included, but the vast majority are those written specifically for young readers.

Because of this bibliography's proposed use as a book selection aid, series of consistently low quality have been omitted. Best-known of these are the Hardy Boys, Tom Swift, Nancy Drew, Cherry Ames, the Bobbsey Twins, the Oz books, and the Five Little Peppers. Books have been evaluated in terms of plot content, depth and believability of characterization, writing style, and book format.

Series are arranged alphabetically by author. Individual titles within each series are arranged by the logical chronological order so that readers may be able to follow desired series in correct sequence.

The authors hope that they have included all existing series, but would greatly appreciate being notified of any error, for correction in the next edition.

The authors also wish to thank most heartily Mrs. Betty Campbell, indexers Roberta Campbell and Anna Myers, typists Linda Bordenkircher, Marge Furrer, and Irene Radabaugh, and general advisor, the venerable and revered John A. Campbell, M.D., for all their many-faceted endeavors. Special thanks go to Mrs. Esther Karnes, Duncan and Kevin Campbell, and Lubomyr R. Wynar for their invaluable aid and encouragement.

FICTION SERIES

ABRASHKIN, Raymond
    See WILLIAMS, Jay

AGLE, Nan, and Ellen Wilson

    THREE BOYS SERIES
1. Three Boys and a Lighthouse.
    New York, Scribner, 1951.
2. Three Boys and the Remarkable Cow.
    New York, Scribner, 1952.
3. Three Boys and a Tugboat.
    New York, Scribner, 1953.
4. Three Boys and a Mine.
    New York, Scribner, 1954.
5. Three Boys and a Train.
    New York, Scribner, 1956.
6. Three Boys and a Helicopter.
    New York, Scribner, 1958.
7. Three Boys and Space.
    New York, Scribner, 1962.
8. Three Boys and H_2O.
    New York, Scribner, 1968.

This series about triplets is uniformly good. The 8 to 10 age group it is designed for will find the large print easy to handle. There is both humor and information dispensed in each book. Especially good for boys.

AIKEN, Joan

9. The Wolves of Willoughby Chase.
    New York, Doubleday, 1963.
10. Black Hearts in Battersea.
    New York, Doubleday, 1964.
11. Nightbirds on Nantucket.
    New York, Doubleday, 1966.
12. The Cuckoo Tree.
    New York, Doubleday, 1971.

    Related book about Owen Hughes:
13. The Whispering Mountain.
    New York, Doubleday, 1969.

AIKEN, Joan—continued

This is an excellent series by Conrad Aiken's daughter. The first two books combine fantasy and humor in a delightful burlesque of nineteenth century England. The third book follows several of the characters across the ocean to America. All are highly recommended.

ALEXANDER, Lloyd

PRYDAIN BOOKS

14. The Book of Three.
    New York, Holt, 1964.
15. The Black Cauldron.
    New York, Holt, 1965.
16. The Castle of Llyr.
    New York, Holt, 1966.
17. Taran Wanderer.
    New York, Holt, 1967.
18. The High King.
    New York, Holt, 1968.

Related books concerning some series characters:

19. The Truthful Harp.
    New York, Holt, 1967.
20. Coll and His White Pig.
    New York, Holt, 1965.

An outstanding series based on Welsh legends. The final volume won the Newbery Award, but the entire series should be read in order to get the benefit of growing up with Taran as he tries to discover who he really is. It can be read and enjoyed by all ages from 11 on up. The two related books are on the 8 to 10 level, with much emphasis placed on Evaline Ness's excellent illustrations.

ALLAN, Mabel Esther (pseud. Jean Estoril)

GARLAND FAMILY SERIES

21. The Ballet Family.
    New York, Criterion, 1966.
22. The Dancing Garlands.
    New York, Criterion, 1968.

ALLAN, Mabel Esther—continued

This series for early teens focuses on the activities of a dancing family. Plots are smooth but may seem contrived to the more perceptive reader. Easy reading for girls who like books that combine career, romance, and foreign locales.

DRINA SERIES
23. Ballet for Drina.
    New York, Vanguard, 1958.
24. Drina's Dancing Year.
    New York, Vanguard, 1958.
25. Drina Dances in Exile.
    London, Hodder, 1959.
26. Drina Dances Again.
    London, Hodder, 1960.
27. Drina Dances in New York.
    London, Hodder, 1961.
28. Drina Dances in Italy.
    New York, Vanguard, 1962.
29. Drina Dances in Paris.
    London, Hodder, 1962.
30. Drina Dances in Madeira.
    London, Hodder, 1963.
31. Drina Dances in Switzerland.
    London, Hodder, 1964.

A young English girl longs to learn ballet, but first must convince her unwilling grandmother to let her take lessons. Later, she goes on to make dancing her career. These books will appeal to girls who enjoy career novels as well as to those who like books about dancing. For ages 10 to 14.

ALMEDINGEN, E. M.

32. Katia.
    New York, Farrar, 1966.
33. Young Mark: The Story of a Venture.
    New York, Farrar, 1968.
34. Fanny.
    New York, Farrar, 1970.
35. Ellen.
    New York, Farrar, 1971.
36. Anna.
    New York, Farrar, 1972.

ALMEDINGEN, E. M.—continued

This impressive series is based on the lives of various members of the author's family. Each gives a fascinating account of a different historical period in different countries. Each is filled with well-rounded, interesting characters. The plots are often slow-moving to create atmosphere, so they are for the more mature readers, from 11 up.

AMERMAN, Lockhart

    JONATHON FLOWER SERIES
37. Guns in the Heather.
    New York, Harcourt, 1963.
38. Cape Cod Casket.
    New York, Harcourt, 1964.
39. The Sly One.
    New York, Harcourt, 1966.

Varied backgrounds, from Cape Cod to Scotland, characterize this mystery-adventure series. Quick-moving plots and witty dialogue make this a better than average selection for the 12 to 16 group.

ANCKARSVARD, Karin

40. The Mysterious Schoolmaster.
    Translated by Annabelle MacMillan
    New York, Harcourt, 1959.
41. The Robber Ghost.
    Translated by Annabelle MacMillan
    New York, Harcourt, 1961.
42. Madcap Mystery.
    Translated by Annabelle MacMillan
    New York, Harcourt, 1962.

These Swedish mysteries, with lively, credible plots, are fortunate to have a good translator, Annabelle MacMillan. Chief characters Michael Olmstedt and Cecilia Acker are well-developed. Popular fare for both boys and girls 9 to 12.

43. Doctor's Boy.
    Translated by Annabelle MacMillan
    New York, Harcourt, 1965.

ANCKARSVARD, Karin—continued

    44. Struggle at Soltuna.
        Translated by Annabelle MacMillan
        New York, Harcourt, 1968.

Set in Sweden during the early twentieth century, these stories tell of the adventures of Jon and Rickard. The stories are warm, with good characterizations and warm family life depicted. For ages 10 to 14.

    AUNT VINNIE SERIES

    45. Aunt Vinnie's Invasion.
        Translated by Annabelle MacMillan
        New York, Harcourt, 1962.
    46. Aunt Vinnie's Victorious Six.
        Translated by Annabelle MacMillan
        New York, Harcourt, 1964.

This series features eccentric Aunt Vinnie and her six charges. Humorous family situations and some adventures are to be found, and—miracle of miracles—each child has a distinct personality.

ARCHER, Marion

    47. There Is a Happy Land.
        Chicago, Whitman, 1963.
    48. Keys for Signe.
        Chicago, Whitman, 1965.

Set in 1865 on a Wisconsin farm, these books follow Signe, a Norwegian immigrant, from her girlhood to maturity, when she moves to the city to earn her living. Her adventures may seem somewhat tame to readers on the 10 to 14 age level.

ARDEN, William

    ALFRED HITCHCOCK AND THE THREE INVESTIGATORS SERIES
        (See also entries under Robert Arthur, M. V. Carey, and Nick West)
    49. Alfred Hitchcock and the Three Investigators in the Mystery of the Moaning Cave. No. 10.
        New York, Random House, 1968.

ARDEN, William—continued

> 50. Alfred Hitchcock and the Three Investigators in the Mystery of the Laughing Shadow. No. 12.
> New York, Random House, 1969.
> 51. Alfred Hitchcock and the Three Investigators in the Secret of the Crooked Cat. No. 13.
> New York, Random House, 1970.
> 52. Alfred Hitchcock and the Three Investigators in the Mystery of the Shrinking House. No. 18.
> New York, Random House, 1972.

The Arden contributions to this series follow the formula of the others. All are adequate, but none is a must for a collection, except that they do attract reluctant readers with the Hitchcock name.

ARMSTRONG, William H.

> 53. Sounder.
> New York, Harper, 1969.
> 54. Sour Land.
> New York, Harper, 1971.

Sounder won the Newbery Award, but its sequel, which follows the nameless Black boy into his old age, is remarkable only for its beautiful descriptions. The characters are passionless and the work, unlike *Sounder* (now a highly-praised film, lacks drama.

ARTHUR, Robert

> ALFRED HITCHCOCK AND THE THREE INVESTIGATORS SERIES
> (See also entries under William Arden, M. V. Carey, and Nick West)
> 55. Alfred Hitchcock and the Three Investigators in the Secret of Terror Castle. No. 1.
> New York, Random House, 1964.
> 56. Alfred Hitchcock and the Three Investigators in the Mystery of the Stuttering Parrot. No. 2.
> New York, Random House, 1964.
> 57. Alfred Hitchcock and the Three Investigators in the Mystery of the Whispering Mummy. No. 3.
> New York, Random House, 1965.
> 58. Alfred Hitchcock and the Three Investigators in the Mystery of the Green Ghost. No. 4.
> New York, Random House, 1965.

ARTHUR, Robert—continued

    59. Alfred Hitchcock and the Three Investigators in the Mystery of the Vanishing Treasure. No. 5.
        New York, Random House, 1966.
    60. Alfred Hitchcock and the Three Investigators in the Secret of Skeleton Island. No. 6.
        New York, Random House, 1966.
    61. Alfred Hitchcock and the Three Investigators in the Mystery of the Fiery Eye. No. 7.
        New York, Random House, 1967.
    62. Alfred Hitchcock and the Three Investigators in the Mystery of the Silver Spider. No. 8.
        New York, Random House, 1967.
    63. Alfred Hitchcock and the Three Investigators in the Mystery of the Screaming Clock. No. 9.
        New York, Random House, 1968.
    64. Alfred Hitchcock and the Three Investigators in the Mystery of the Talking Skull. No. 11.
        New York, Random House, 1969.

These are all popular with the children, but are of no great literary merit. Certainly possession of the entire series is not necessary. They do appeal to reluctant readers, however.

ARUNDEL, Honor

    65. The High House.
        New York, Hawthorne, 1968.
    66. Emma's Island.
        New York, Hawthorne, 1970.

When a young English girl's parents die, she goes to live with her artistic but eccentric aunt and uncle in Scotland. Her adjustment takes longer than usual in this plot situation, since she only begins to find security in the second book, when they take a summer trip to an island. A well-written series, this will be a good bet for readers 11 to 14.

ASHFORD, Jeffrey

    DICK KNOX SERIES
    67. Grand Prix Monaco.
        New York, Putnam, 1968. (Putnam Sports Shelf)

ASHFORD, Jeffrey—continued

    68. Grand Prix Germany.
        New York, Putnam, 1970. (Putnam Sports Shelf)

These are rather hackneyed novels with racetrack settings. Plots are predictable, characters dull, dialogue stilted. The only redeeming feature lies in the on-track sequences, which bear some stamp of authenticity. The subject matter and vocabulary may make this a good bet for boys grades 5 on up.

AVERILL, Esther

    JENNY LINSKY SERIES
    69. The Cat Club.
        New York, Harper, 1944.
    70. The School for Cats.
        New York, Harper, 1947.
    71. Jenny's First Party.
        New York, Harper, 1948.
    72. Jenny's Moonlight Adventure.
        New York, Harper, 1949.
    73. When Jenny Lost Her Scarf.
        New York, Harper, 1951.
    74. Jenny's Adopted Brothers.
        New York, Harper, 1952.
    75. How the Brothers Joined the Cat Club.
        New York, Harper, 1953.
    76. Jenny's Birthday Book.
        New York, Harper, 1954.
    77. Jenny Goes to Sea.
        New York, Harper, 1957.
    78. Jenny's Bedside Book.
        New York, Harper, 1959.
    79. The Hotel Cat.
        New York, Harper, 1969.
    80. Captains of the City Streets.
        New York, Harper, 1972.

Related story:
    81. The Fire Cat.
        New York, Harper, 1960.

AVERILL, Esther—continued

Miss Jenny Linsky is a small, ultra-feminine black cat. Her adventures are related with humor and charm that should appeal to children from 5 to 9. Some members of this series are written on a picture book level, while others—like *Jenny Goes to Sea* and *The Hotel Cat*—are intended for grades 2 to 4.

BAKER, Charlotte

    KINDNESS CLUB SERIES

      82. The Best of Friends.
          New York, McKay, 1966.
      83. The Kittens and the Cardinals.
          New York, McKay, 1969.

The members of the Kindness Club seek to prevent cruelty to animals, as well as rescue creatures in trouble. This leads them into some adventures, but more often into preciousness or preachiness.

BAKER, Elizabeth

    TAMMY SERIES

      84. Tammy Camps Out.
          Boston, Houghton Mifflin, 1958.
      85. Tammy Climbs Pyramid Mountain.
          Boston, Houghton Mifflin, 1962.
      86. Tammy Goes Canoeing.
          Boston, Houghton Mifflin, 1966.
      87. Tammy Camps in the Rocky Mountains.
          Boston, Houghton Mifflin, 1970.

This series is about a young girl and her various adventures in the wilderness as she goes camping. The stories are told with good humor. Tammy is a very appealing character, and her independence and adventures should appeal to girls, especially in view of the accent on women's liberation today.

BAKER, Margaret J.

      88. The Shoe Shop Bears.
          New York, Farrar, 1965.
      89. Hannibal and the Bears.
          New York, Farrar, 1966.

BAKER, Margaret J.—continued

    90. Bears Back in Business.
        New York, Farrar, 1967.
    91. Hi-Jinks Joins the Bears.
        New York, Farrar, 1969.

The first book in this series is a delightful fantasy about bears who come alive in a shoe shop. Dialogue is humorous, the situations captivating. A real gem. Unfortunately, none of the others quite reaches its quality. They all are readable, however. For ages 7 to 11.

HOMER THE TURTLE SERIES

    92. Homer the Tortoise.
        New York, Prentice, 1949.
    93. Homer Sees the Queen.
        New York, Prentice, 1953.
    94. Homer Goes to Stratford.
        New York, Prentice, 1958.

A series for those 8- to 12-year-olds who enjoy talking animals. Homer not only abounds in good humor, but is also very cultured. His visit to Stratford to visit Shakespeare's home may even pique the curiosity of some young readers to delve farther into the life and works of the Bard.

BALL, Zachary (pseud.)
    See MASTERS, Kelly

BARD, Mary

    95. Best Friends.
        Philadelphia, Lippincott, 1955.
    96. Best Friends in Summer.
        Philadelphia, Lippincott, 1960.
    97. Best Friends at School.
        Philadelphia, Lippincott, 1961.

The best friends of the title are CoCo and Susie. Both girls are winsome and their adventures should appeal to girls 8 to 10. Not, however, on a par with Lovelace or Sachs.

BARRETT, William

> 98. The Lilies of the Field.
> New York, Doubleday, 1962.
> 99. The Glory Tent.
> New York, Doubleday, 1967.

Although written for adults, both of these slim volumes are simple enough reading for grades 6 and up. With the added attraction of being an award-winning film, *Lilies of the Field* in particular could be used with reluctant readers.

BARTOS-HOPPNER, Barbara

> 100. The Cossacks.
> Translated by Stella Humphries.
> New York, Walck, 1963.
> 101. Save the Khan.
> Translated by Stella Humphries.
> New York, Walck, 1964.

This series, set in the time of Ghengis Khan, improved as it progressed. The first volume, while colorful and highly detailed, sometimes suffered from over-complexity of plot. The second volume is a stirring, well-sustained narrative. Both, however, are worth having for the excellent historical background.

BATES, Esther

> MARILDA SERIES
> 102. Marilda's House.
> New York, McKay, 1956.
> 103. Marilda and the Witness Tree.
> New York, McKay, 1957.
> 104. Marilda and the Bird of Time.
> New York, McKay, 1960.

When young Marilda is orphaned, she and her friends raise the money to enable her to keep her house. The later books follow her growing-up period. For girls 12 to 14.

BEATTY, Jerome

MATTHEW LOONEY SERIES

105. Matthew Looney's Voyage to the Earth.
New York, Scott, 1961.
106. Matthew Looney's Invasion of the Earth.
New York, Scott, 1965.
107. Matthew Looney in the Outback.
New York, Scott, 1969.
108. Matthew Looney and the Space Pirates.
New York, Scott, 1972.

Lighthearted spoofs on science and civilization with deeper levels of meaning for those who care to look. For readers 10 to 14.

BELL, Margaret

MONROE FAMILY SERIES

109. Watch for a Tall White Sail.
New York, Morrow, 1948.
110. The Totem Casts a Shadow.
New York, Morrow, 1949.
111. Love Is Forever.
New York, Morrow, 1954.
112. Daughter of Wolf House.
New York, Morrow, 1957.

These four books concern the Monroe family's adventures in Alaska. For the most part, the characters are well presented and the plots believable, except for the third offering, which suffers from an overly-sentimental style with respect to both plot and characters.

BENARY-ISBERT, Margot

ANNEGRET SERIES

113. Shooting Star.
Translated by Richard and Clara Winston
New York, Harcourt, 1954.
114. Blue Mystery.
Translated by Richard and Clara Winston
New York, Harcourt, 1957.

BENARY-ISBERT, Margot—continued

    115. A Time to Love.
          Translated by Joyce Emerson
          New York, Harcourt. 1962.

These stories follow the adventures of Annegret from her childhood into her early teens. All benefit from a smoothly beautiful descriptive style and strong characterizations.

    LECHOW FAMILY SERIES

    116. The Ark.
          Translated by Richard and Clara Winston
          New York, Harcourt, 1953.
    117. Rowan Farm.
          Translated by Richard and Clara Winston
          New York, Harcourt, 1954.
    118. Castle on the Border.
          Translated by Richard and Clara Winston
          New York, Harcourt, 1956.

This excellent series deals with the Lechow family's readjustment after World War II. Especially outstanding are the strong characterizations.

BENEDICT, Dorothy

    119. Pagan the Black.
          New York, Pantheon, 1960.
    120. Fabulous.
          New York, Pantheon, 1961.
    121. Bandoleer.
          New York, Pantheon, 1963.

These three horse stories vary in quality. *Pagan* is somewhat sentimental and melodramatic, but the other two are quite absorbing and would be popular with girls from 9 to 12.

BERNA, Paul

    GABY SERIES

    122. The Horse Without a Head.
          Translated by John Buchanan-Brown
          New York, Pantheon, 1958.

BERNA, Paul—continued

    123. The Street Musician.
        Translated by John Buchanan-Brown
            London, Bodley Head, 1960 (1956).
    124. The Mystery of St. Salgue.
        Translated by John Buchanan-Brown
            New York, Pantheon, 1963.

Related books about Inspector Sinet:

    125. The Clue of the Black Cat.
        Translated by John Buchanan-Brown
            New York, Pantheon, 1965.
    126. A Truckload of Rice.
        Translated by John Buchanan-Brown
            New York, Pantheon, 1968.
    127. Mule on the Expressway.
        Translated by John Buchanan-Brown
            New York, Pantheon, 1968.

Here are mysteries with a French setting. The plots are well-developed, characterizations are strong, and the style is witty. Better than average mystery fare.

BEST, Herbert

    DESMOND SERIES

    128. Desmond's First Case.
        New York, Viking, 1961.
    129. Desmond the Dog Detective.
        New York, Viking, 1962.
    130. Desmond and the Peppermint Ghost.
        New York, Viking, 1965.
    131. Desmond and Dog Friday.
        New York, Viking, 1968.

This is a humorous, well-done, easy-to-read mystery series about Desmond the dog detective. Good for boys and reluctant readers in the 8 to 10 age bracket.

BIALK, Elisa

    MARTY SERIES

    132. Marty.
        Cleveland, World, 1953.

BIALK, Elisa—continued

    133. Marty Goes to Hollywood.
        Cleveland, World, 1954.
    134. Marty on the Campus.
        Cleveland, World, 1956.

This series about a hometown girl reporter who eventually winds up in journalism school at Northwestern is no longer in print. Characters and dialogue are too old-fashioned to appeal to girls today.

    TIZZ SERIES

    135. Tizz.
        Chicago, Childrens, 1955.
    136. Tizz Takes a Trip.
        Chicago, Childrens, 1956.
    137. Tizz Plays Santa Claus.
        Chicago, Childrens, 1957.
    138. Tizz and Co.
        Chicago, Childrens, 1958.
    139. Tizz on a Pack Trip.
        Chicago, Childrens, 1961.
    140. Tizz Is a Cowpony.
        Chicago, Childrens, 1961.
    141. Tizz on a Horse Farm.
        Chicago, Childrens, 1964.
    142. Tizz in Cactus Country.
        Chicago, Childrens, 1964.
    143. Tizz in Texas.
        Chicago, Childrens, 1966.
    144. Tizz on a Trail Ride.
        Chicago, Childrens, 1966.
    145. Tizz in the Canadian Rockies.
        Chicago, Childrens, 1968.
    146. Tizz at the Stampede.
        Chicago, Childrens, 1968.
    147. Tizz at the Fiesta.
        Chicago, Childrens, 1970.
    148. Tizz South of the Border.
        Chicago, Childrens, 1971.

The Tizz books, concerning the adventures of a horse, are all very similar. Written for ages 8 to 10, they use large print and colorful illustrations which add to the appeal for younger readers. Certainly the entire series is not a must, but a few on hand would be good for this age level.

BINNS, Archie

    149. Sea Pup.
        New York, Hawthorne, 1954.
    150. Sea Pup Again.
        New York, Hawthorne, 1965.

Clint Barlow befriends a baby white seal he finds near his home on the Puget Sound. Clint and his sea pup have various escapades, all of which should be fun, in this slightly different animal story.

BJARNHOF, Karl

    151. The Stars Grow Pale.
        Translated by Naomi Walford
        New York, Knopf, 1958.
    152. The Good Light.
        Translated by Naomi Walford
        New York, Knopf, 1960.

This semi-autobiographical series tells of a boy in pre-World War I Denmark. Although partially blind, he develops an interest in the arts. Eventually he becomes totally blind. Told compellingly, in wrenching detail, this series is best given to the mature reader, from age 14 on up.

BODEN, Hilda

    MOLLY STEWART SERIES
    153. The Mystery of Castle Croome.
        New York, McKay, 1966.
    154. The Mystery of Island Keep.
        New York, McKay, 1968.
    155. Storm over Wales.
        New York, McKay, 1970.

Romance mystery and melodrama prevail here, with foreign settings.

BOND, Michael

    PADDINGTON SERIES
    156. A Bear Called Paddington.
        Boston, Houghton Mifflin, 1960.

BOND, Michael—continued

    157. Paddington Helps Out.
          Boston, Houghton Mifflin, 1961.
    158. More About Paddington.
          Boston, Houghton Mifflin, 1962.
    159. Paddington at Large.
          Boston, Houghton Mifflin, 1963.
    160. Paddington Marches On.
          Boston, Houghton Mifflin, 1965.
    161. Paddington at Work.
          Boston, Houghton Mifflin, 1967.
    162. Paddington Goes to Town.
          Boston, Houghton Mifflin, 1968.
    163. Paddington Takes the Air.
          Boston, Houghton Mifflin, 1971.
    164. Paddington Abroad.
          Boston, Houghton Mifflin, 1972.

Paddington, the English bear, is a delight for the 8 to 10 set, or even for older children. For the most part, the series is highly enjoyable, with word play that is fun even for adults. The third offering, *More About Paddington*, is rather repetitious of the first, but it is still fun. Adding to the enjoyment are Peggy Fortnum's drawings.

    THURSDAY SERIES

    165. Here Comes Thursday.
          New York, Lothrop, 1967.
    166. Thursday Rides Again.
          New York, Lothrop, 1969.
    167. Thursday Ahoy!
          New York, Lothrop, 1970.

For the same age group as Paddington, this series has not been as popular in this country. Still, it is enjoyable and worth having, and could be suggested to devoted Paddington followers.

BONHAM, Frank

    OAK STREET BOYS CLUB SERIES

    168. The Mystery of the Fat Cat.
          New York, Dutton, 1968.
    169. The Nitty Gritty.
          New York, Dutton, 1968.

BONHAM, Frank—continued

This mystery series with a ghetto setting, by the author of *Burma Rifles*, follows the adventures of the Oak Street Boys Club as they unravel various mysteries. Well done, especially good for boys 9 to 12.

BOOTH, Esma

    KALENA SERIES
    170. Kalena.
        New York, McKay, 1958.
    171. Kalena and Sana.
        New York, McKay, 1962.

This series is about the daughter of an African chief in the Belgian Congo. She must eventually make a choice between the narrow but familiar life of the village and the learning she so wishes to obtain. The picture of African life is fascinating and Kalena's problems should be familiar to girls from 11 to 14.

BOSTON, L. M.

    GREEN KNOWE SERIES
    172. The Children of Green Knowe.
        New York, Harcourt, 1954.
    173. The Treasure of Green Knowe.
        New York, Harcourt, 1958.
    174. The River at Green Knowe.
        New York, Harcourt, 1959.
    175. A Stranger at Green Knowe.
        New York, Harcourt, 1961.
    176. An Enemy at Green Knowe.
        New York, Harcourt, 1964.

This is an excellent series, all the members of which are equally good. They are fantasies, yet set in the world of reality. The child Tolly meets the children of long ago who once inhabited Green Knowe. Characterizations are strong, the settings are vivid. One of the best of the series is the last book, which is a suspense fantasy.

BOTHWELL, Jean

    177. The Thirteenth Stone.
        New York, Harcourt, 1946.
    178. The Search for a Golden Bird.
        New York, Harcourt, 1956.

This well-written series is set in India. In the course of searching for his true identity, Jivan learns the secrets of other mysteries as well. For grades 5 to 8.

    179. The Promise of the Rose.
        New York, Harcourt, 1958.
    180. The Defiant Bride.
        New York, Harcourt, 1969.

Set in sixteenth century Kashmir, this series has the advantage of an exotic background and customs to lend interest. The young heroine insists, against custom, that she be allowed to select her own husband. The role of women in society in the past may interest future Women's Libbers.

BRAENNE, Berit

    181. Trina Finds a Brother.
        Translated by Evelyn Ramsden
            New York, Harcourt, 1962.
    182. Little Sister Tai-Mi.
        Translated by Evelyn Ramsden
            New York, Harcourt, 1964.

These stories are about seagoing Trina and her family. In their travels they meet and adopt a Korean girl and an Arab boy. The tales are told with humor and sympathy and should transmit the idea of brotherhood to young readers from 8 to 12.

BRAND, Christianna (pseud.)
    See LEWIS, Mary Christianna

BRENT, Stuart

    MR. TOAST SERIES
    183. The Strange Disappearance of Mr. Toast.
        New York, Viking, 1964.

BRENT, Stuart—continued

 184. Mr. Toast and the Woolly Mammoth.
   New York, Viking, 1966.
 185. Mr. Toast and the Secret of Ghost Hill.
   New York, Viking, 1970.

The hero of these mystery-adventures is a golden retriever of surpassing intelligence. He's the serious counterpart to Desmond. For dog lovers from 9 to 12.

BRINK, Carol Ryrie

 186. Family Grandstand.
   New York, Viking, 1952.
 187. Family Sabbatical.
   New York, Viking, 1956.

A charming series about the adventures of a professor's family. Told with warmth and humor, very refreshing.

BRINLEY, Bertrand

 MAD SCIENTISTS SERIES

 188. The Mad Scientists' Club.
   Philadelphia, Macrae Smith, 1965.
 189. The New Adventures of the Mad Scientists' Club.
   Philadelphia, Macrae Smith, 1968.

Seven young scientists keep their town hopping with their experiments. Fun for boys especially, from 9 to 12.

BROOKS, Walter

 FREDDY THE PIG SERIES

 190. Freddy the Detective.
   New York, Knopf, 1932.
 191. Freddy the Politician.
   New York, Knopf, 1939.
 192. Freddy's Cousin Weedly.
   New York, Knopf, 1940.
 193. Freddy and the Ignoramus.
   New York, Knopf, 1941.

BROOKS, Walter—continued

194. Freddy and the Perilous Adventure.
     New York, Knopf, 1942.
195. Freddy and the Bean Home News.
     New York, Knopf, 1943.
196. Freddy and Mr. Camphor.
     New York, Knopf, 1944.
197. Freddy and the Popinjay.
     New York, Knopf, 1945.
198. Freddy and the Pied Piper.
     New York, Knopf, 1946.
199. Freddy the Magician.
     New York, Knopf, 1947.
200. Freddy Goes Camping.
     New York, Knopf, 1948.
201. Freddy Plays Football.
     New York, Knopf, 1949.
202. Freddy Goes to Florida.
     New York, Knopf, 1949.
203. Freddy the Cowboy.
     New York, Knopf, 1950.
204. Freddy Goes to the North Pole.
     New York, Knopf, 1951.
205. Freddy Rides Again.
     New York, Knopf, 1951.
206. Freddy the Pilot.
     New York, Knopf, 1952.
207. Freddy and Freginald.
     New York, Knopf, 1952.
208. Freddy and the Space Ship.
     New York, Knopf, 1953.
209. Freddy and the Men from Mars.
     New York, Knopf, 1954.
210. Freddy and the Baseball Team from Mars.
     New York, Knopf, 1955.
211. Freddy and Simon the Dictator.
     New York, Knopf, 1956.
212. Freddy and the Flying Saucer Plans.
     New York, Knopf, 1957.
213. Freddy and the Dragon.
     New York, Knopf, 1958.

BROOKS, Walter—continued

    Related to the series:

    214. The Collected Poems of Freddy the Pig.
        New York, Knopf, 1953.

This massive series has been popular with several generations of children and is still being reissued. On the whole, the series is good, nonsensical fun for children from 8 to 10.

BROWN, Palmer

    ANNA LAVINIA SERIES

    215. Beyond the Pawpaw Trees.
        New York, Harper, 1954.
    216. The Silver Nutmeg.
        New York, Harper, 1956.

This series mixes fact with fantasy. The second book is better than the first, which has an adult, sophisticated humor that is above the level of children who would be reading it.

BUCHANAN, William (pseud.)
    See BUCK, William Ray

BUCK, William Ray (pseud. William Buchanan)

    217. Dr. Anger's Island.
        New York, Abelard-Schuman, 1961.
    218. The Ghost of Dagger Bay.
        New York, Abelard-Schuman, 1963.
    219. Eagle's Paradise.
        New York, Abelard-Schuman, 1964.

The first offering is a well-plotted mystery; the second also is suspenseful, with good characterizations, but the dialogue is unnatural.

BURCH, Robert

    220. D.J.'s Worst Enemy.
        New York, Viking, 1965.

BURCH, Robert—continued

>221. Renfroe's Christmas.
>New York, Viking, 1968.

Mr. Burch is well known for his fine novels set in Georgia. These two are no exception. They follow the everyday situations of D.J.'s family, with a strong emphasis on the rural, regional atmosphere. The dialogue is natural, the humor unforced, and the characters very warm. For readers from 8 to 12.

BURMAN, Ben Lucien

>CATFISH BEND SERIES
>222. High Water at Catfish Bend.
>New York, Taplinger, 1952.
>223. Seven Stars for Catfish Bend.
>New York, Taplinger, 1956.
>224. The Owl Hoots Twice at Catfish Bend.
>New York, Taplinger, 1961.
>225. Blow a Wild Bugle for Catfish Bend.
>New York, Taplinger, 1967.

These stories about the animals at Catfish Bend are enjoyable for the 8- to 10-year-olds, although the last one is less imaginative and rather stilted.

BURTON, Hester

>226. Castors Away!
>New York, Crowell, 1963.
>227. The Henchmans at Home.
>New York, Crowell, 1970.

This family series is set in Victorian England. The first, which is a continuous narrative, is superior to the second, which covers separate incidents concerning each character in separate chapters. Ms. Burton maintains consistency of character and sense of time and place throughout both novels.

BUTLER, Beverly

>228. Light a Single Candle.
>New York, Dodd, 1964.
>229. Gift of Gold.
>New York, Dodd, 1972.

BUTLER, Beverly—continued

This series is about Cathy Wheeler, who discovers at the age of 14 that she will be blind. The first book deals with her reaction to this news and her attempt to adapt to her problem. The second book deals with the possibility that her sight may be restored and explores the various emotional problems that go along with such a tense situation. This is very sympathetically treated, and is based on some experiences in the author's own life. A very popular item for girls 9 to 14.

BUTTERWORTH, W. E.

    230. Fast Green Car.
        New York, Norton, 1965.
    231. Return to Racing.
        New York, Grosset, 1971.

Butterworth's usual exciting fare, with a racetrack setting. The hero in this one is Tony Fletcher. A good bet for reluctant readers. For ages 10 to 16.

CADELL, Elizabeth

    232. The Lark Shall Sing.
        New York, Morrow, 1955.
    233. Six Impossible Things.
        New York, Morrow, 1961.

For a change, a teenage romance with style. Ms. Cadell lends her very polished talents to the tale of the orphaned Wayne children and their attempts to stay together. First rate.

CALHOUN, Mary

    KATIE JOHN SERIES

    234. Katie John.
        New York, Harper, 1960.
    235. Depend on Katie John.
        New York, Harper, 1961.
    236. Honestly, Katie John.
        New York, Harper, 1963.

This is a very good series for girls 8 to 12. The tomboyish doings of Katie John are realistic enough to be both identifiable and humorous for girls the same age, and both adults and children are portrayed believably.

CAMERON, Eleanor

>MR. BASS OR MUSHROOM PLANET SERIES
>
>237. The Wonderful Flight to the Mushroom Planet.
>   Boston, Little, 1954.
>238. Stowaway to the Mushroom Planet.
>   Boston, Little, 1956.
>239. Mr. Bass's Planetoid.
>   Boston, Little, 1958.
>240. A Mystery for Mr. Bass.
>   Boston, Little, 1960.
>241. Time and Mr. Bass.
>   Boston, Little, 1967.

This is a highly original blend of science fiction and magic that should appeal to both boys and girls. The plots are fast-moving, and the last volume is especially good in its treatment of the struggle between good and evil.

>TOM AND JENNIFER SERIES
>
>242. The Terrible Churnadryne.
>   Boston, Little, 1959.
>243. The Mysterious Christmas Shell.
>   Boston, Little, 1961.

Another good series by this author, this one combining reality and fantasy in a delicate way. Both have adventure and humor, and the second one is a mystery as well. Outstanding illustrations by Beth and Joe Krush add to the books.

CAMPBELL, Bruce (pseud.)
>See EPSTEIN, Samuel

CAREY, M. V.

>ALFRED HITCHCOCK AND THE THREE INVESTIGATORS SERIES
>   (See also William Arden, Robert Arthur, and Nick West)
>
>244. Alfred Hitchcock and the Three Investigators in the
>   Mystery of the Flaming Footprints. No. 16.
>   New York, Random, 1971.
>245. Alfred Hitchcock and the Three Investigators in the
>   Mystery of the Singing Serpent. No. 17.
>   New York, Random, 1972.

Much the same as the others in the series. The only recommendation is that they are unfailingly popular and are useful with reluctant readers.

CARLSON, Natalie Savage

    246. The Half Sisters.
          New York, Harper, 1970.
    247. Luvvy and the Girls.
          New York, Harper, 1971.

This new series gives a good picture of convent life in the early twentieth century, with Ms. Carlson's usual capable style, but the second book is rather slow-moving, and the subject matter is rather narrow for the 9-to-12 age group for which it was written.

    ORPHELINES SERIES

    248. The Happy Orpheline.
          New York, Harper, 1957.
    249. A Brother for the Orphelines.
          New York, Harper, 1959.
    250. A Pet for the Orphelines.
          New York, Harper, 1962.
    251. The Orphelines in the Enchanted Castle.
          New York, Harper, 1964.

These stories of French orphans are all delightful and lively. The humor is sophisticated, sometimes reflecting on the social behavior of adults. Very well done.

CARROLL, Ruth

    TATUM FAMILY SERIES OR TOUGH ENOUGH SERIES

    252. Beanie.
          New York, Walck, 1953.
    253. Tough Enough.
          New York, Walck, 1954.
    254. Tough Enough's Trip.
          New York, Walck, 1956.
    255. Tough Enough's Pony.
          New York, Walck, 1957.
    256. Tough Enough and Sassy.
          New York, Walck, 1958.
    257. Tough Enough's Indians.
          New York, Walck, 1960.
    258. Runaway Pony, Runaway Dog.
          New York, Walck, 1963.

This series is simply written, with large type and illustrations, so it should be ideal for reluctant readers from 8 to 10. The stories are a humorous treatment of Beanie and her dog and pony. The sixth book of the series is not up to the level of the others, but it is still acceptable.

CAUDILL, Rebecca

BONNIE SERIES

259. Happy Little Family.
    New York, Winston, 1947.
260. The Schoolhouse in the Woods.
    New York, Winston, 1949.
261. Up and Down the River.
    New York, Winston, 1951.
262. Schoolroom in the Parlor.
    New York, Winston, 1959.

This charming series follows young Bonnie from the time when she is not yet old enough to go to school until she enters, and her adventures there. Ms. Caudill writes in her always charming style.

CAVANNA, Betty (pseud. Elizabeth Headley)

DIANE SERIES

263. A Date for Diane.
    Philadelphia, Macrae Smith, 1946.
264. Diane's New Love.
    Philadelphia, Macrae Smith, 1955.
265. Toujours Diane.
    Philadelphia, Macrae Smith, 1957.

This series has mercifully been allowed to go out of print. It bears no relation to today's teenager, and has been included because, to date, it is Ms. Cavanna's only series.

CHASTAIN, Madye Lee

266. Dark Treasure.
    New York, Harcourt, 1954.
267. Emmy Keeps a Promise.
    New York, Harcourt, 1964.
268. Magic Island.
    New York, Harcourt, 1964.

These books about Lissa, Emmy, and Dodie are wholesome, heartwarming stories with good characterizations. Good for girls 9 to 12.

CHASTAIN, Madye Lee—continued

    FRIPSEY SERIES

    269. Bright Days.
        New York, Harcourt, 1952.
    270. Fripsey Summer.
        New York, Harcourt, 1953.
    271. Fripsey Fun.
        New York, Harcourt, 1955.
    272. Leave It to the Fripseys.
        New York, Harcourt, 1957.

This older series about the adventures of the Fripsey family is still very popular with young readers from 9 to 12.

CHAUNCY, Nan

    BADGE LORENNY SERIES

    273. Tiger in the Bush.
        New York, Watts, 1961.
    274. Devil's Hill.
        New York, Watts, 1960.
    275. The Roaring 40.
        New York, Watts, 1963.

These books, set in Tasmania, benefit from an unusual setting. Characters and family relationships are presented strongly. The Australian vernacular is somewhat hard to follow, but the last book includes a helpful glossary of terms.

CHRISTENSEN, Gardell

    276. Buffalo Kill.
        New York, Nelson, 1959.
    277. The Buffalo Robe.
        New York, Nelson, 1960.
    278. Buffalo Horse.
        New York, Nelson, 1961.

This series follows a young Indian boy through his growing-up period and also deals with the growing conflict between Indians and white men. For ages 10 to 14.

CHRISTOPHER, John

    279. The White Mountains.
        New York, Macmillan, 1967.
    280. The City of Gold and Lead.
        New York, Macmillan, 1967.
    281. The Pool of Fire.
        New York, Macmillan, 1968.

This is an excellent series of science fiction adventures, dealing with good and evil in future times. Good for boys in particular.

    282. The Prince in Waiting.
        New York, Macmillan, 1970.
    283. Beyond the Burning Lands.
        New York, Macmillan, 1971.
    284. The Sword of the Spirits.
        New York, Macmillan, 1972.

Another top-notch series with implications about technology, honor, peace and freedom. The second entry is the weakest member of the trilogy.

CLARE, Helen, pseud. (Clarke, Pauline)

    285. Five Dolls in a House.
        New York, Prentice, 1965.
    286. Five Dolls and Their Friends.
        New York, Prentice, 1967.
    287. Five Dolls in the Snow.
        New York, Prentice, 1967.
    288. Five Dolls and the Monkey.
        New York, Prentice, 1967.
    289. Five Dolls and the Duke.
        New York, Prentice, 1968.

This series is by the author of *The Return of the Twelves*. While the contents are not as thought-provoking, still they will be of interest to girls from 8 to 12. The owner of a doll house magically becomes doll-sized. The dolls in her doll house think of her as their landlady and the young heroine and the dolls have quite a few adventures together. Each doll has her own individual personality and each is quite charming.

CLARK, Electa

    CASEY McKEE SERIES

    290. The Dagger, the Fish, and Casey McKee.
        New York, McKay, 1955.
    291. Spanish Gold and Casey McKee.
        New York, McKay, 1956.

A first-rate mystery series. Ms. Clark combines rollicking action with amusing characters and well-developed plots.

CLARKE, Pauline
    See CLARE, Helen (pseud.)

CLEARY, Beverly

    HENRY HUGGINS SERIES

    292. Henry Huggins.
        New York, Morrow, 1950.
    293. Ellen Tebbits.
        New York, Morrow, 1951.
    294. Henry and Beezus.
        New York, Morrow, 1952.
    295. Otis Spofford.
        New York, Morrow, 1953.
    296. Henry and Ribsy.
        New York, Morrow, 1954.
    297. Beezus and Ramona.
        New York, Morrow, 1955.
    298. Henry and the Paper Route.
        New York, Morrow, 1957.
    299. Henry and the Clubhouse.
        New York, Morrow, 1962.
    300. Ribsy.
        New York, Morrow, 1964.
    301. Ramona the Pest.
        New York, Morrow, 1968.

As large as it is, this series has been uniformly excellent. The books deal with the adventures of Henry and his friends, his dog, Ribsy, and problems with little sister Ramona. All the characters are well portrayed; the situations are believable and humorous. Print is large, and Louis Darling's lively drawings capture the humor of the text.

CLEARY, Beverly—continued

RALPH THE MOUSE SERIES

302. The Mouse and the Motorcycle.
New York, Morrow, 1965.
303. Runaway Ralph.
New York, Morrow, 1970.

Ralph the Mouse resembles *Stuart Little* in his humorous adventures, but there is enough original about him to warrant reading. Ms. Cleary couples strict attention to detail with wildly improbable settings to make her fantasy seem real. Good for the 8 to 10 age bracket.

CLEAVER, Vera, and Bill Cleaver

ELLEN GRAE SERIES

304. Ellen Grae.
Philadelphia, Lippincott, 1967.
305. Lady Ellen Grae.
Philadelphia, Lippincott, 1968.

Related to the series:

306. Grover.
Philadelphia, Lippincott, 1970.

This series, about Ellen Grae's problems in growing up, has excellent characterizations. The plots, while having moments of humor, are basically serious. Treated with sympathy, they are quite touching.

CLEWES, Dorothy

HADLEY FAMILY SERIES

307. The Mystery of the Scarlet Daffodil.
New York, Coward, 1953.
308. The Mystery of the Blue Admiral.
New York, Coward, 1954.
309. The Mystery on Rainbow Island.
New York, Coward, 1956.
310. The Mystery of the Jade Green Cadillac.
New York, Coward, 1958.
311. The Mystery of the Lost Tower Treasure.
New York, Coward, 1960.

CLEWES, Dorothy—continued

    312. The Mystery of the Singing Strings.
        New York, Coward, 1961.
    313. The Mystery of the Midnight Smugglers.
        New York, Coward, 1964.

A better-than-average mystery series for the 10 to 12 year olds. The Hadley children are lively, distinct individuals, and the plots are intriguing.

COLVER, Anne

    MOLLY-O AND PIP SERIES

    314. Borrowed Treasure.
        New York, Knopf, 1959.
    315. Secret Castle.
        New York, Knopf, 1960.

Two mysteries for younger readers. The first involves a "borrowed" horse and so should appeal to both horse- and mystery-lovers.

    BREAD-AND-BUTTER SERIES

    316. Bread-and-Butter Indian.
        New York, Holt, 1964.
    317. Bread-and-Butter Journey.
        New York, Holt, 1970.

This series, set in pioneer days, is based on true stories. These slender volumes, with good illustrations by Garth Williams, will be appealing to girls from 8 to 12.

CONE, Molly

    MISHMASH SERIES

    318. Mishmash.
        Boston, Houghton Mifflin, 1962.
    319. Mishmash and the Substitute Teacher.
        Boston, Houghton Mifflin, 1963.
    320. Mishmash and the Sauerkraut Mystery.
        Boston, Houghton Mifflin, 1965.
    321. Mishmash and Uncle Looey.
        Boston, Houghton Mifflin, 1968.

CONE, Molly—continued

This is a funny, appealing series about the adventures of the dog, Mishmash. Good for both boys and girls 8 to 10. The third entry is not as humorous and cohesive as the others, however.

CONSTANT, Alberta

>MILLER FAMILY SERIES
>
>322. Those Miller Girls!
>   New York, Crowell, 1965.
>323. The Motoring Millers.
>   New York, Crowell, 1969.

This popular series follows the adventures of the Miller family in Kansas in 1910. A charming picture of life then is an extra attraction.

COOMBS, Patricia

>DORRIE SERIES
>
>324. Dorrie's Magic.
>   New York, Lothrop, 1962.
>325. Dorrie and the Blue Witch.
>   New York, Lothrop, 1964.
>326. Dorrie's Play.
>   New York, Lothrop, 1965.
>327. Dorrie and the Weather Box.
>   New York, Lothrop, 1966.
>328. Dorrie and the Witch Doctor.
>   New York, Lothrop, 1967.
>329. Dorrie and the Wizard's Spell.
>   New York, Lothrop, 1968.
>330. Dorrie and the Haunted House.
>   New York, Lothrop, 1970.
>331. Dorrie and the Birthday Eggs.
>   New York, Lothrop, 1971.
>332. Dorrie and the Goblin.
>   New York, Lothrop, 1972.

A charming series for younger readers about the adventures of a good little witch. The vocabulary is easy and the subject matter popular and humorous.

COPELAND, Helen

    DUNCAN McKENNA SERIES
333. Duncan's World.
    New York, Crowell, 1967.
334. This Snake Is Good.
    New York, Crowell, 1968.

An exciting, well-written series with lots of information about nature and animals. Young Duncan has many adventures both with his pets and with animals he meets in the wild. A good one for boys 8 to 10.

CORBETT, Scott

335. Tree House Island.
    Boston, Little, 1959.
336. Cutlass Island.
    Boston, Little, 1962.

These are both well-constructed mysteries, with a swift pace and good humor. The plot of the second one does strain credulity, but they will appeal to boys 9 to 12.

    ROGER TEARLE SERIES
337. The Case of the Gone Goose.
    Boston, Little, 1966.
338. The Case of the Fugitive Firebug.
    Boston, Little, 1969.
339. The Case of the Ticklish Tooth.
    Boston, Little, 1971.

These lighthearted adventures of Inspector Roger Tearle are handled with Mr. Corbett's special blend of the ridiculous and reality. For boys and reluctant readers.

    TRICK BOOKS
340. The Lemonade Trick.
    Boston, Little, 1960.
341. The Mailbox Trick.
    Boston, Little, 1961.
342. The Disappearing Dog Trick.
    Boston, Little, 1963.
343. The Limerick Trick.
    Boston, Little, 1964.

CORBETT, Scott—continued

    344. The Baseball Trick.
        Boston, Little, 1965.
    345. The Turnabout Trick.
        Boston, Little, 1967.
    346. The Hairy Horror Trick.
        Boston, Little, 1969.
    347. The Hateful Plateful Trick.
        Boston, Little, 1971.

This hilarious series is especially appealing to boys because of its mischievous hero, Kerby Maxwell. Mr. Corbett mixes real boys and situations with fantasy and magic. The third and latest entries lack the spontaneity of the others, but the rest of the series is a must.

    348. Diamonds Are Trouble.
        New York, Holt, 1967. (Pacesetter Books)
    349. Diamonds Are More Trouble.
        New York, Holt, 1969. (Pacesetter Books)

This series is intended for the reluctant reader on the junior-senior high level. The author's slick handling of these mystery-adventures should have high appeal.

CORDELL, Alexander

    350. The White Cockade.
        New York, Viking, 1970.
    351. Witches' Sabbath.
        New York, Viking, 1970.
    352. The Healing Blade.
        New York, Viking, 1971.

This trilogy follows the adventures of John Regan during the Irish Revolution of 1798. This should be especially interesting in view of the current troubles in Ireland. Young readers may get an insight into longstanding bones of contention.

CRAIG, Margaret

    353. Three Who Met.
        New York, Crowell, 1958.

CRAIG, Margaret—continued

    354. Now That I'm Sixteen.
        New York, Crowell, 1959.

The problems of Beth Hiller, an outstanding student, are here detailed with insight and realism. What was realism 12 years ago may have little appeal today, but this series is not as outdated as some written at the same period. For girls 10 to 16.

CRISP, Frank

    355. The Haunted Reef.
        New York, Coward, 1950.
    356. The Sea Robbers.
        New York, Coward, 1953.
    357. The Java Wreckmen.
        New York, Coward, 1956.
    358. The Manila Menfish.
        New York, Coward, 1957.
    359. The Sea Ape.
        New York, Coward, 1959.
    360. The Sanguman.
        New York, Clark McCutcheon, 1965.

Jim Cartwright and Dirk Rogers are the heroes of this adventure series. Plots are exciting, characters generally well drawn, and the deep sea diving background should intrigue boys 11 to 16.

CROWLEY, Maude

    AZOR SERIES

    361. Azor.
        New York, Walck, 1948.
    362. Azor and the Blue-eyed Cow.
        New York, Walck, 1951.
    363. Tor and Azor.
        New York, Walck, 1955.

    Related to the series:

    364. Pringle and the Lavendar Goat.
        New York, Walck, 1960.

CROWLEY, Maude—continued

These stories may seem a trifle old-fashioned to children today, but they do present a warm, humorous picture of life in New England. The second entry is still valuable as a Christmas story.

CUNNINGHAM, Julia

    365. Burnish Me Bright.
        New York, Pantheon, 1970.
    366. Far in the Day.
        New York, Pantheon, 1972.

Ms. Cunningham's sensitive portrayal of the mute Auguste, his training in the art of the mime, and his subsequent encounters with evil, is for the special reader. The second book does not stand well on its own.

CURRY, Jane Louise

    367. Beneath the Hill.
        New York, Harcourt, 1967.
    368. The Daybreakers.
        New York, Harcourt, 1970.
    369. Over the Sea's Edge.
        New York, Harcourt, 1971.

Ms. Curry has created a series that combines the best elements of fantasy, adventure, and philosophy. The books should be read sequentially for the total impact. Highly recommended.

DAHL, Roald

    370. Charlie and the Chocolate Factory.
        New York, Knopf, 1964.
    371. Charlie and the Great Glass Elevator.
        New York, Knopf, 1972.

The first member of this series is quite well known, having been made into the film, *Willie Wonka and the Chocolate Factory*. It has universal appeal in the story of the poor boy whose good manners and good upbringing reap rich rewards. The second book features Charlie and friend Willie on a trip into outer space. They meet many odd characters, who add to the humor and the suspense.

DARINGER, Helen

    372. Pilgrim Kate.
        New York, Harcourt, 1949.
    373. Country Cousin.
        New York, Harcourt, 1951.
    374. Debbie of the Green Gate.
        New York, Harcourt, 1956.

These three stories are about different girls who come from the Scrooby Congregation in Leyden, Holland. These girls and their families must decide whether to move to America to escape religious persecution. Their decision is told in these stories with great warmth. Characters are well developed, plots are exciting, and the independent girls should still appeal to readers today.

DE LEEUW, Adele

    RUGGED DOZEN SERIES
    375. The Rugged Dozen.
        New York, Macmillan, 1956.
    376. The Rugged Dozen Abroad.
        New York, Macmillan, 1960.

This series about the adventures of a troop of Girl Scouts would seem to have a rather limited appeal, although Ms. De Leeuw turns in her usual competent performance.

DEL REY, Lester

    377. Step to the Stars.
        New York, Holt, 1954.
    378. Mission to the Moon.
        New York, Holt, 1956.

This is standard science fiction fare by one of the better writers in the field. Jim Stanley fights sabotage on several planets, as well as on starships. Good adventure for the buffs.

DEMING, Dorothy

    379. Penny Marsh: Public Health Nurse.
        New York, Dodd, 1938.

DEMING, Dorothy—continued

    380. Penny Marsh: Supervisor.
        New York, Dodd, 1939.
    381. Ginger Lee: War Nurse.
        New York, Dodd, 1942.
    382. Penny Marsh and Ginger Lee: Wartime Nurses.
        New York, Dodd, 1943.
    383. Penny and Pam: Nurse and Cadet.
        New York, Dodd, 1944.
    384. Pam Wilson: Registered Nurse.
        New York, Dodd, 1946.
    385. Penny Marsh Finds Adventure.
        New York, Dodd, 1954.
    386. Penny Marsh, R.N.: Director of Nurses.
        New York, Dodd, 1960.

This antique series, which follows the development of three career nurses, has little relevance to nursing or girls today. Unfortunately, the only recent series on nursing is Laklan's. With only two entries there, and the continued interest of readers in nursing, this series, along with Sue Barton, continues to attract readers. For teenage die-hards.

    WENDY BRENT SERIES

    387. Curious Calamity in Ward 8.
        New York, Dodd, 1954.
    388. Strange Disappearance from Ward 2.
        New York, Dodd, 1956.
    389. Mysterious Discovery in Ward K.
        New York, Dodd, 1959.
    390. Baffling Affair in the County Hospital.
        New York, Dodd, 1962.

Somewhat more up to date is this mystery series with a nursing background. This should appeal to both mystery and career fans, as well as reluctant readers.

DENNEBORG, H. M.

    391. Jan and the Wild Horse.
        Translated by Emile Capouya
        New York, McKay, 1958.
    392. The Only Horse for Jan.
        Translated by Emile Capouya
        New York, McKay, 1961.

DENNEBORG, H. M.—continued

These Danish horse stories are told with humor and originality. The outstanding characteristic here is the treatment of characters to show all their human foibles. The translation does not detract from the books.

DERLETH, August

    393. The Moon Tenders.
          New York, Duell, 1958.
    394. The Mill Creek Irregulars.
          New York, Duell, 1959.
    395. The Pinkertons Ride Again.
          New York, Duell, 1960.

Characters Steve and Sim solve various mysteries in these exciting, if sometimes improbable, stories. The writing style is good; the books should appeal to boys 9 to 12.

DICK, Trella

    TORNADO JONES SERIES

    396. Tornado Jones.
          Chicago, Follett, 1953.
    397. Tornado Jones on Sentinal Mountain.
          Chicago, Follett, 1955.
    398. Tornado's Big Year.
          Chicago, Follett, 1956.

This series concerns the mystery-adventures of a young basketball player. There is some attention to the problems of junior-high-schoolers, but this may seem somewhat dated now. Ages 10 to 14.

DICKENS, Monica

    399. The House at World's End.
          New York, Doubleday, 1970.
    400. Summer at World's End.
          New York, Doubleday, 1972.

The Fielding children are left on their own as their parents go on a trip. This type of situation, with youngsters fending for themselves, has proven to be a very workable plot basis. Ms. Dickens has expanded it into a projected series.

DICKENS, Monica—continued

The style of writing is tightknit and the adventures of the children are more plausible than in similar books, primarily those of Gertrude Warner. For the 9 to 12 set.

DICKINSON, Peter

>THE CHANGES SERIES
>
>401. The Weathermonger.
>>Boston, Little, 1969.
>402. Heartsease.
>>Boston, Little, 1969.
>403. The Devil's Children.
>>New York, Gollancz, 1970.

An unusual science fiction series in which the characters, who live in an anti-machine society, travel through time, and so visit various periods of earth's history. Very well done.

DICKSON, Gordon

>ROBBY HOENIG SERIES
>
>404. Secret Under the Sea.
>>New York, Holt, 1960.
>405. Secret Under Antarctica.
>>New York, Holt, 1963.
>406. Secret Under the Caribbean.
>>New York, Holt, 1964.

Science fiction mysteries in different settings—they provide information as well as action. A good way to teach the reluctant reader indirectly.

DINES, Glen

>407. The Mysterious Machine.
>>New York, Macmillan, 1957.
>408. The Fabulous Flying Bicycle.
>>New York, Macmillan, 1960.

Here is a humorous science-fiction series which features outlandish inventions and far-fetched plots that should appeal to fans of Danny Dunn and Sid Fleischman. For reader 8 to 12.

DIVINE, David

    409. The Stolen Seasons.
        New York, Crowell, 1970.
    410. Three Red Flares.
        New York, Crowell, 1972.

These stories are about Mig and Peter Manson and their friend Clint Hammond. The tales are a combination mystery-adventure. The unusual thing about them is that they combine an interest in archaeology and English history with the adventure. This makes them a better-than-average bet for the young reader from 8 to 12.

DONOVAN, Edward J.

    411. Adventure on Ghost River.
        New York, Duell, 1960.
    412. Adventure on Sunset Trail.
        New York, Duell, 1961.

These adventure novels are set in the north woods of Ontario. The plots are fast moving and the details of life in the rough should interest readers.

DOUGLAS, James McM.

    413. Hunger for Racing.
        New York, Putnam, 1967. (Putnam Sports Shelf)
    414. Racing to Glory.
        New York, Putnam, 1969. (Putnam Sports Shelf)
    415. The Twelve-Cylinder Screamer.
        New York, Putnam, 1970. (Putnam Sports Shelf)
    416. Drag Race Driver.
        New York, Putnam, 1971. (Putnam Sports Shelf)

Another car-racing adventure series by Butterworth, produced under a pseudonym. Although the plots are run-of-the-mill, they are handled with humor and the racing sequences are not only exciting but also have a ring of authenticity. For readers 11 to 16.

DU BOIS, William Pene

    OTTO SERIES
    417. Otto at Sea.
        New York, Viking, 1958.

DU BOIS, William Pene—continued

    418. Otto in Texas.
        New York, Viking, 1959.
    419. Otto in Africa.
        New York, Viking, 1961.
    420. Otto and the Magic Potatoes.
        New York, Viking, 1970.

Marvelous tall tales for 8 to 10 year olds, these stories about the giant dog Otto are great fun, with the added attraction of Mr. Du Bois's effervescent drawings.

    421. The Alligator Case.
        New York, Harper, 1965.
    422. The Horse in the Camel Suit.
        New York, Harper, 1967.

Both of these books are enjoyable mysteries, with an unnamed boy detective as the hero. For readers 8 to 10, the second book may be too complicated, but the drawings are, as always, a delight.

DU JARDIN, Rosamond

    TOBEY HEYDON SERIES

    423. Practically Seventeen.
        Philadelphia, Lippincott, 1949.
    424. Class Ring.
        Philadelphia, Lippincott, 1951.
    425. Boy Trouble.
        Philadelphia, Lippincott, 1953.
    426. The Real Thing.
        Philadelphia, Lippincott, 1956.
    427. Wedding in the Family.
        Philadelphia, Lippincott, 1958.
    428. One of the Crowd.
        Philadelphia, Lippincott, 1961.

Although in danger of becoming outdated, Ms. Du Jardin's natural dialogue and realistic handling of teenage problems keeps this series a perennial favorite with readers.

    429. Double Date.
        Philadelphia, Lippincott, 1952.

DU JARDIN, Rosamond—continued

    430. Double Feature.
          Philadelphia, Lippincott, 1953.
    431. Showboat Summer.
          Philadelphia, Lippincott, 1955.
    432. Double Wedding.
          Philadelphia, Lippincott, 1959.

The heroines here are twins whose activities are followed through college into marriage. Still applicable today are their attempts to assert their individuality and independence.

    MARCY SERIES

    433. Wait for Marcy.
          Philadelphia, Lippincott, 1950.
    434. Marcy Catches Up.
          Philadelphia, Lippincott, 1952.
    435. A Man for Marcy.
          Philadelphia, Lippincott, 1954.
    436. Senior Prom.
          Philadelphia, Lippincott, 1957.

Unlike Ms. Du Jardin's other two series, this one does not hold up well. Its treatment of high school romance is dated. Only for die-hard fans.

DUNCAN, Jane

    CAMERON FAMILY SERIES

    437. The Camerons on the Train.
          New York, St. Martin's, 1963.
    438. The Camerons on the Hills.
          New York, St. Martin's, 1964.
    439. The Camerons at the Castle.
          New York, St. Martin's, 1964.
    440. The Camerons Calling.
          New York, St. Martin's, 1966.
    441. Camerons Ahoy!
          New York, St. Martin's, 1968.

Set in Scotland, this mystery series has the advantage of locale and the involvement of all the family members in unraveling the problem. The relationships among the family are treated with understanding. For grades 7 to 10.

DUNSING, Dorothy

    442. War Chant.
        New York, Longmans, 1954.
    443. The Seminole Trail.
        New York, Longmans, 1956.

This series is historical fiction, set in Florida in the 1830s against the backdrop of the Seminole wars. This unusual setting should be especially of interest due to the resurgence of interest in Indians and their history.

EAGER, Edward

    444. Magic or Not?
        New York, Harcourt, 1959.
    445. The Well-Wishers.
        New York, Harcourt, 1960.

The first volume of this series with Laura and James as the chief characters is very well done, with a fresh plot, and a lively mystery. Unfortunately, the second suffers from a mixed-up plot, too much preaching, and adult philosophy, as well as literary allusions not in the field of a young reader's knowledge.

    446. Half Magic.
        New York, Harcourt, 1954.
    447. Knight's Castle.
        New York, Harcourt, 1956.
    448. Magic by the Lake.
        New York, Harcourt, 1957.
    449. The Time Garden.
        New York, Harcourt, 1958.

This is by far the most successful series of the two. It is a delightful fantasy spoof, again about a group of children who discover many magic devices, including a coin that only grants half their wish. All show imagination and humor and can be read on more than one level.

EBY, Lois (pseud. Patrick Lawson)

    450. Star-Crossed Stallion.
        New York, Dodd, 1954.
    451. Star-Crossed Stallion's Big Chance.
        New York, Dodd, 1957.

EBY, Lois—continued

This is a typical horse story, a rather watered-down version of Walter Farley with nothing to raise it above mediocrity.

EIFERT, Virginia

    452. The Buffalo Trace.
        New York, Dodd, 1955.
    453. Out of the Wilderness.
        New York, Dodd, 1956.
    454. Three Rivers South.
        New York, Dodd, 1953.
    455. With a Task Before Me.
        New York, Dodd, 1958.
    456. New Birth of Freedom.
        New York, Dodd, 1959.

This acclaimed series presents a fictionalized account of Abraham Lincoln's life beginning before his birth and continuing to his death. This series could lead a reader to Sandburg's fine biography or into other books about this period of United States history. Highly recommended.

EMERY, Anne

    DINNY GORDON SERIES
    457. Dinny Gordon, Freshman.
        Philadelphia, Macrae Smith, 1959.
    458. Dinny Gordon, Sophomore.
        Philadelphia, Macrae Smith, 1961.
    459. Dinny Gordon, Junior
        Philadelphia, Macrae Smith, 1964.
    460. Dinny Gordon, Senior.
        Philadelphia, Macrae Smith, 1965.

This series about a college girl who is (miraculously) more interested in archaeology than in boys will appeal to girls 12 to 14.

    461. The Popular Crowd.
        Philadelphia, Westminster, 1961.
    462. The Losing Game.
        Philadelphia, Westminster, 1965.

EMERY, Anne—continued

Young Sue Morgan is faced with various ethical problems in these two books. She must cope with cheating, snobbery, and necking, among other things. Unfortunately, the author's treatment is superficial and her pat solutions will not be bought by today's teenager.

> 463. County Fair.
> Philadelphia, Macrae Smith, 1953.
> 464. Hickory Hill.
> Philadelphia, Macrae Smith, 1955.
> 465. Sweet Sixteen.
> Philadelphia, Macrae Smith, 1956.

Another typical teenage series, this time featuring country girl Jane Ellison.

> 466. First Love, True Love.
> Philadelphia, Westminster, 1956.
> 467. First Orchid for Pat.
> Philadelphia, Westminster, 1957.
> 468. First Love, Farewell.
> Philadelphia, Westminster, 1958.

Yet another teenage romance-cum-career series. Pat Marlowe seeks a career in the theater, meets a young man, goes away to school, and eventually breaks her engagement. Standard fare for readers.

ENGDAHL, Sylvia

> 469. Enchantress from the Stars.
> New York, Atheneum, 1970.
> 470. The Far Side of Evil.
> New York, Atheneum, 1971.

Here is a most unusual series, which combines science fiction with mythology and fantasy. Highly recommended for teenagers on up.

ENRIGHT, Elizabeth

> GONE-AWAY SERIES
> 471. Gone-Away Lake.
> New York, Harcourt, 1957.
> 472. Return to Gone-Away.
> New York, Harcourt, 1961.

ENRIGHT, Elizabeth—continued

This is a delightful series, well written, with vigor and humor coupled with a touch of fantasy.

EPSTEIN, Samuel, and Beryl Epstein

    TIMOTHY PENNY SERIES
    473. Jackknife for a Penny
        New York, Coward, 1958.
    474. Change for a Penny.
        New York, Coward, 1959.

Set during the Revolutionary War, these are rousing good tales with plenty of action, strong characterizations, and plotting. This should rouse the interest of those who are not particularly interested in American history. For ages 10 to 14.

(Pseud. Bruce Campbell)

    KEN HOLT SERIES
    475. The Secret of Skeleton Island.
        New York, Grosset, 1949.
    476. The Riddle of the Stone Elephant.
        New York, Grosset, 1949.
    477. The Black Thumb Mystery.
        New York, Grosset, 1950.
    478. The Clue of the Marked Claw.
        New York, Grosset, 1950.
    479. The Clue of the Coiled Cobra.
        New York, Grosset, 1951.
    480. The Secret of Hangman's Inn.
        New York, Grosset, 1951.
    481. The Mystery of the Iron Box.
        New York, Grosset, 1952.
    482. The Clue of the Phantom Car.
        New York, Grosset, 1953.
    483. The Mystery of the Galloping Horse.
        New York, Grosset, 1954.
    484. The Mystery of the Green Flame.
        New York, Grosset, 1955.
    485. The Mystery of the Grinning Tiger.
        New York, Grosset, 1956.

EPSTEIN, Samuel, and Beryl Epstein (pseud. Bruce Campbell)—continued

    486. The Mystery of the Vanishing Magician.
          New York, Grosset, 1956.
    487. The Mystery of the Shattered Glass.
          New York, Grosset, 1958.
    488. The Mystery of the Invisible Enemy.
          New York, Grosset, 1959.
    489. The Mystery of Gallows Cliff.
          New York, Grosset, 1960.
    490. The Clue of the Silver Scorpion.
          New York, Grosset, 1961.
    491. The Mystery of the Plumed Serpent.
          New York, Grosset, 1962.
    492. The Mystery of the Sultan's Scimitar.
          New York, Grosset, 1963.

This series is on a par with Nancy Drew and The Hardy Boys. It would not have been included except to indicate an additional series by the author of a better-quality series—in this case, Samuel Epstein.

ERDMAN, Loula

    PIERCE FAMILY SERIES

    493. The Wind Blows Free.
          New York, Dodd, 1952.
    494. Wide Horizon.
          New York, Dodd, 1956.
    495. The Good Land.
          New York, Dodd, 1959.

These books, about the adventures of the pioneering Pierce family, are on a borderline age level. Some of the subject matter is more suited to teenagers, but the writing style is on a fairly young level. For a mature younger reader, this would be a good historical series to recommend.

ERWIN, Betty

    496. Aggie, Maggie, and Tish.
          Boston, Little, 1965.
    497. Where's Aggie?
          Boston, Little, 1967.

ERWIN, Betty—continued

Three magical little old ladies enchant the Eliot children, who try to puzzle out how much of the fun is *real* magic. Lighthearted fun for those 9 to 12.

ESTES, Eleanor

    498. The Alley.
        New York, Harcourt, 1964.
    499. The Tunnel of Hugsy Goode.
        New York, Harcourt, 1972.

These two books about a special tunnel in a college town are told with Ms. Estes' usual gentle affection. They are blends of mystery and fantasy, with strong characterizations. For all readers 9 to 12.

    PYE FAMILY SERIES

    500. Ginger Pye.
        New York, Harcourt, 1951.
    501. Pinky Pye.
        New York, Harcourt, 1958.

Ginger Pye, about a new puppy in the Pye family, won the Newbery Award. Its sequel treats the Pyes with the same spontaneous warmth and humor. An outstanding series.

ESTORIL, Jean (pseud.)
    See ALLAN, Mabel Esther

FABER, Nancy

    502. Cathy at the Crossroads.
        Philadelphia, Lippincott, 1962.
    503. Cathy's Secret Kingdom.
        Philadelphia, Lippincott, 1963.

Young Cathy becomes involved in several mysteries, including ferreting out her stepmother's secret. For readers 9 to 12.

FARLEY, Walter

    BLACK STALLION SERIES

    504. The Black Stallion.
        New York, Random House, 1941.
    505. The Black Stallion Returns.
        New York, Random House, 1945.
    506. Son of the Black Stallion.
        New York, Random House, 1947.
    507. The Black Stallion and Satan.
        New York, Random House, 1949.
    508. The Blood Bay Colt.
        New York, Random House, 1950.
    509. The Black Stallion's Filly.
        New York, Random House, 1952.
    510. The Black Stallion Revolts.
        New York, Random House, 1953.
    511. The Black Stallion's Sulky Colt.
        New York, Random House, 1954.
    512. The Black Stallion's Courage.
        New York, Random House, 1956.
    513. The Black Stallion's Mystery.
        New York, Random House, 1957.
    514. The Black Stallion and Flame.
        New York, Random House, 1960.
    515. The Black Stallion Challenged.
        New York, Random House, 1964.
    516. The Black Stallion's Ghost.
        New York, Random House, 1969.
    517. The Black Stallion and the Girl.
        New York, Random House, 1971.

This series is a well-done set of horse stories that, like the Freddy books, have been popular with girls for several generations. Certainly the entire set is not necessary, but any would be a good choice on a limited budget.

    ISLAND STALLION SERIES

    518. The Island Stallion.
        New York, Random House, 1948.
    519. The Island Stallion's Fury.
        New York, Random House, 1951.
    520. The Island Stallion Races.
        New York, Random House, 1955.

FARLEY, Walter—continued

    521. The Black Stallion and Flame.
        New York, Random House, 1960.

The final book of this series links it to the Black Stallion series. Again, here are popular, well-written horse stories for girls 9 to 12.

FARMER, Penelope

    522. The Summer Birds.
        New York, Harcourt, 1962.
    523. Emma in Winter.
        New York, Harcourt, 1966.
    524. Charlotte Sometimes.
        New York, Harcourt, 1969.

These are fantasy allegories written on several levels, both as fantasy and adventure, with some philosophy thrown in. The third book of the series is exceptionally fine, with its depiction of the changes in identity between the one girl who moves from her present into the past when she becomes a different person during the First World War, and the changes that this imposes upon her. Recommended for girls especially, 9 to 14.

FAULKNOR, Cliff

    525. The White Calf.
        Boston, Little, 1965.
    526. The White Peril.
        Boston, Little, 1966.

Set in the 1850s, this series deals with the problems of Eagle Child, an Indian youth who must adjust to the white man's territorial expansion. For readers 10 and up.

FELTON, Ronald Oliver
    See WELCH, Ronald, pseud.

FIFE, Dale

    LINCOLN SERIES
    527. Who's in Charge of Lincoln?
        New York, Coward, 1965.

FIFE, Dale—continued

    528. What's New, Lincoln?
         New York, Coward, 1970.
    529. What's the Prize, Lincoln?
         New York, Coward, 1971.

Here are some easy readers for the 8 to 10 group. The hero is a Negro boy named Lincoln who has various delightful adventures in and out of school.

FITZGERALD, John

GREAT BRAIN SERIES

    530. The Great Brain.
         New York, Dial, 1967.
    531. More Adventures of the Great Brain.
         New York, Dial, 1969.
    532. Me and My Little Brain.
         New York, Dial, 1971.
    533. The Great Brain at the Academy.
         New York, Dial, 1972.

The Great Brain, full of ideas and plots as he is, constantly gets himself and his friends in trouble. Witty and tender, this series is great fun, especially for boys. The third entry charmingly relates the Great Brain's little brother's entry into the world of plans and schemes.

FITZHUGH, Louise

    534. Harriet the Spy.
         New York, Harper, 1964.
    535. The Long Secret.
         New York, Harper, 1965.

Harriet the Spy is well on its way to becoming a classic. The story of a little girl who takes notes (pretty nasty ones, too) about her friends and neighbors presents its characters' good and bad sides—all too rarely done in children's books. Its sequel is primarily about her friend Beth, although Harriet is a peripheral character. Somewhat controversial because it deals with menstruation, it is done in good taste.

FLEISCHMAN, Sid

McBROOM SERIES

536. McBroom Tells the Truth.
    New York, Norton, 1966.
537. McBroom and the Big Wind.
    New York, Norton, 1967.
538. McBroom's Ear.
    New York, Norton, 1969.
539. McBroom's Ghost.
    New York, Grosset, 1971.
540. McBroom's Zoo.
    New York, Grosset, 1972.

All five are excellent tall tales as told by McBroom, truly hilarious. Especially good for reluctant readers.

FLORY, Jane

541. Peddler's Summer.
    Boston, Houghton Mifflin, 1960.
542. Mist on the Mountain.
    Boston, Houghton Mifflin, 1966.

These books depict the life of young Amanda Scoville 100 years ago. The picture of family relationships and the way of living during that period is a gem of Americana. For readers 9 to 12.

FORSTER, Logan

543. Desert Storm.
    New York, Dodd, 1955.
544. Mountain Stallion.
    New York, Dodd, 1958.
545. Tamarlane.
    New York, Dodd, 1959.

These three books are about three separate horses that were trained by the same Indian boy. As adventures and horse stories they are adequate, but the character of the boy does not grow from one book to the next.

FOSTER, John

> MARCO SERIES
>
> 546. Marco and the Tiger.
>   New York, Dodd, 1967.
> 547. Marco and the Sleuth Hound.
>   New York, Dodd, 1969.
> 548. Marco and That Curious Cat.
>   New York, Dodd, 1970.

All exciting new series about the mystery-adventures of the boy Marco. Good for boys 9 to 12.

FRANZEN, Nils-Olaf

> AGATON SAX SERIES
>
> 549. Agaton Sax and the Diamond Thieves.
>   Translated by Evelyn Ramsden
>   New York, Delacorte, 1967.
> 550. Agaton Sax and the Scotland Yard Mystery.
>   Translated by Evelyn Ramsden
>   New York, Delacorte, 1969.
> 551. Agaton Sax and the Incredible Max Brothers.
>   Translated by Evelyn Ramsden
>   New York, Delacorte, 1970.

Here is a semi-satirical series about an obnoxiously know-it-all detective. The author treats it all in the style of a deadpan farce, which comes off quite well in the translation. Sax recalls a famous counterpart in Sherlock Holmes. Good fun for mystery buffs and others with a like sense of humor.

FROST, Frances

> WINDY FOOT SERIES
>
> 552. Windy Foot at the County Fair.
>   New York, McGraw, 1947.
> 553. Sleigh Bells for Windy Foot.
>   New York, McGraw, 1948.
> 554. Maple Sugar for Windy Foot.
>   New York, McGraw, 1950.
> 555. Fireworks for Windy Foot.
>   New York, McGraw, 1956.

FROST, Frances—continued

These stories about young Toby Clark and his pony, Windy Foot, explore life in the New England country, from county fairs to maple sugar gathering. For 8 to 12 year olds.

FYSON, J. G.

556. The Three Brothers of Ur.
     New York, Coward, 1966.
557. The Journey of the Eldest Son.
     New York, Coward, 1967.

Set in ancient Mesopotamia, these novels gather their strength from the detailed depiction of the beliefs and customs of these people. There is adventure here, and the books could be used in conjunction with social studies, but outside of that the appeal is liable to prove limited.

GALLICO, Paul

JEAN-PIERRE SERIES

558. The Day the Guinea Pig Talked.
     New York, Doubleday, 1963.
559. The Day Jean-Pierre Was Pignapped.
     New York, Doubleday, 1964.
560. The Day Jean-Pierre Went Round the World.
     New York, Doubleday, 1965.
561. The Day Jean-Pierre Joined the Circus.
     New York, Watts, 1969.

This series about the adventures of a talking guinea pig pushes credulity a bit too far. Mr. Gallico becomes overly sentimental and his characterizations and plots are both entirely too mannered. For grades 2 to 4.

GARNER, Alan

562. The Weirdstone.
     New York, Watts, 1960.
563. The Moon of Gomrath.
     New York, Walck, (1963) 1967.

This is a well-received series which combines Scandinavian, Celtic, and Welsh mythology. The style of writing is superb. Characterizations are strong. Scenes

GARNER, Alan—continued

and action bring the feeling of a creeping horror. Because the stories are not fast moving, they may be more for the special reader, but they are certainly first-rate fare.

GARNETT, Eve

>564. The Family from One-End Street.
>   New York, Vanguard, (1939) 1960.
>565. Further Adventures of the Family from One-End Street.
>   New York, Vanguard, 1956.
>566. Holiday at the Dew Drop Inn, a One-End Story.
>   New York, Vanguard, 1962.

The first member of this series is a Carnegie Medal winner, and explores the adventures of the Ruggles family in England. The second and third members are not as well written as the first, although the second book does have some hilarious passages and the characters are old friends. Unfortunately, the third book contains many references to the first book, so readers who have not read it will be at a disadvantage.

GILMAN, Robert Charn

>RHADA SERIES
>
>567. The Rebel of Rhada.
>   New York, Harcourt, 1968.
>568. The Navigator of Rhada.
>   New York, Harcourt, 1969.
>569. Starkahn of Rhada.
>   New York, Harcourt, 1970.

These science fiction books could be appealing to boys 10 to 12, but the plots are complicated, and the second book suffers from two-dimensional characters. Characters and situations in the first book are also alluded to without explanation, so they should be read in order.

GIPSON, Fred

>570. Old Yeller.
>   New York, Harper, 1956.

GIPSON, Fred—continued

      571. Savage Sam.
           New York, Harper, 1962.

Both outstanding dog stories set in pioneer days. These books will be popular not only with elementary age readers, but also with teenagers. Reluctant readers may also be attracted by the fact that these were made into Disney movies.

GODDEN, Rumer

      572. Miss Happiness and Miss Flower.
           New York, Viking, 1961.
      573. Little Plum.
           New York, Viking, 1963.

Any girl who loves dolls will love these charming stories. The first book is about two Japanese dolls, but it can also be read as a Christmas story. Appended to it are building plans for a doll house. The second book is a delightful suspense story, especially strong for its characters, who are presented with both their good and their bad sides.

GOVAN, Christine

      HACKBERRY STREET SERIES
      574. Number 5 Hackberry Street.
           Cleveland, World, 1964.
      575. Return to Hackberry Street.
           Cleveland, World, 1967.

This series is intended for slightly older readers than the previous one. It concerns a young girl in a small town in Tennessee at the turn of the century. The aspects of small town life at that time are enjoyably explored.

      576. The Curious Clubhouse.
           Cleveland, World, 1967.
      577. The Trash Pile Treasure.
           Cleveland, World, 1970.

Yet another mystery series by Ms. Govan. This one concerns the adventures of the Carpenter children. Their characterizations are better developed than most heroes of such series. While not all of Ms. Govan's efforts are essential to a collection, some would certainly be in order.

GOVAN, Christine, and Emmy West

LOOKOUT CLUB SERIES

578. The Mystery at Shingle Rock.
New York, Sterling, 1955.
579. The Mystery at the Mountain Face.
New York, Sterling, 1956.
580. The Mystery at the Shuttered Hotel.
New York, Sterling, 1956.
581. The Mystery at Moccasin Bend.
New York, Sterling, 1957.
582. The Mystery at the Indian Hide-Out.
New York, Sterling, 1957.
583. The Mystery at the Deserted Mill.
New York, Sterling, 1958.
584. The Mystery of the Vanishing Stamp.
New York, Sterling, 1958.
585. The Mystery at the Haunted House.
New York, Sterling, 1959.
586. The Mystery at Plum Nelly.
New York, Sterling, 1959.
587. The Mystery at Fearsome Lake.
New York, Sterling, 1960.
588. The Mystery at Rock City.
New York, Sterling, 1960.
589. The Mystery at the Snowed-In Cabin.
New York, Sterling, 1961.
590. The Mystery of the Dancing Skeleton.
New York, Sterling, 1962.
591. The Mystery at Ghost Lodge.
New York, Sterling, 1963.
592. The Mystery at the Weird Ruins.
New York, Sterling, 1964.
593. The Mystery at the Echoing Cave.
New York, Sterling, 1965.

These better-than-average mysteries for the younger reader (grades 3 to 5) contain more action and plot plausibility than is normal for series in this genre. A good bet for reluctant readers.

GRAHAM, Lorenz

DAVID WILLIAMS SERIES

594. South Town.
Chicago, Follett, 1958.

GRAHAM, Lorenz—continued

    595. North Town.
          Chicago, Follett, 1965.
    596. Whose Town.
          Chicago, Follett, 1969.

This is a strong series about a Negro boy, David Williams, and the problems he encounters as he grows up in various places. The first book is for 10 to 12 year olds, but the others are for more mature readers.

GRIFFITH, Valeria

    597. Jenny, the Fire Maker.
          Philadelphia, Lippincott, 1963.
    598. A Ride for Jenny.
          Philadelphia, Lippincott, 1964.

Young Jenny is always in trouble. Either her clumsiness causes problems or her bright ideas do. Nonetheless, she manages to win a prize at her summer camp in Colorado. All right reading for those 8 to 12.

GRIPE, Maria

    HUGO AND JOSEPHINE SERIES

    599. Josephine.
        Translated by Paul Britten Austin.
          New York, Delacorte Press, 1970 (1961).
    600. Hugo and Josephine.
        Translated by Paul Britten Austin
          New York, Delacorte Press, 1969 (1962).
    601. Hugo.
        Translated by Paul Britten Austin
          New York, Delacorte Press, 1970 (1966).

Young Hugo, a self-possessed, knowing lad, befriends Josephine and teachers her not to be afraid of being different. A good presentation of the ups and downs of boy-girl friendships.

HAHN, Emily

    FRANCIE SERIES
    602. Francie.
          New York, Watts, 1951.

HAHN, Emily—continued

  603. Francie Again.
    New York, Grosset, 1953.
  604. Francie Comes Home.
    New York, Watts, 1956.

This teenage series follows Francie as she studies and travels abroad. She then becomes a fashion buyer, then marries. Although somewhat dated, the series is still readable and may yet appeal to today's teenagers.

HALACY, Dan

 ETHAN STRONG SERIES

  605. Ethan Strong: Strike and Fight Back.
    New York, McGraw, 1968.
  606. Ethan Strong: Watch by the Sea.
    New York, McGraw, 1969.

This series is about undercover agent Ethan Strong, who works with Naval Intelligence. The plots are generally preposterous, the characterizations vapid. The series is included here only to indicate that this prolific author has produced one.

HALL, Elizabeth

  607. Phoebe Snow.
    Boston, Houghton Mifflin, 1968.
  608. Stand Up, Lucy.
    Boston, Houghton Mifflin, 1971.

Young Lucy, who is rather mature-looking for her age, masquerades as her mother in order to go to the exposition in St. Louis at the turn of the century. Such enterprise by a young girl was unheard of in those days. In the second book, Lucy becomes even more adventurous as she becomes involved with the Suffragette movement through her aunt. Her independence will appeal greatly to today's girls. For grades 4 through 6.

HALL, Marjorie

  609. Star Island.
    New York, Funk and Wagnalls, 1953.

HALL, Marjorie—continued

   610. Star Island Again.
     New York, Funk and Wagnalls, 1955.
   611. Three Stars for Star Island.
     New York, Funk and Wagnalls, 1958.

Carolyn Winthrop and several of her friends (both male and female) become camp counselors for several successive summers on Star Island. These books detail their trials and joys. Many of the sentiments will seem outdated to the teenage reader at whom they are aimed. Not a necessary addition to the collection.

   612. Whirl of Fashion.
     Philadelphia, Westminster, 1961.
   613. To Paris and Love.
     Philadelphia, Westminster, 1962.

Another teenage career series, this one follows Felicia Larcom as she studies fashion design in school, then goes to France to practice her craft. An all right choice for those interested in career books.

HAMRE, Leif

   614. Leap into Danger.
     Translated by Evelyn Ramsden
      New York, Harcourt, 1959.
   615. Edge of Disaster.
     Translated by Evelyn Ramsden
      New York, Harcourt, 1960.
   616. Perilous Wings.
     Translated by Evelyn Ramsden
      New York, Harcourt, 1961.

These books are exciting mysteries with foreign settings that would be recommended for boys 9 to 12. The chief characters, Geir and Peter, are Danish pilots.

HARRIS, Rosemary

   617. The Moon in the Cloud.
     New York, Macmillan, 1970.
   618. The Shadow on the Sun.
     New York, Macmillan, 1970.

HARRIS, Rosemary—continued

    619. The Bright and Morning Star.
         New York, Macmillan, 1972.

Ms. Harris generally writes about unusual people and subjects, and this series is no exception. Set in Egypt, this series has the mood, atmosphere, and strong characterizations that are her hallmark. A blend of comedy, fantasy, and adventure, this series is for the unusual reader from 10 to 13.

HAUGAARD, Erik

    620. Hakon of Rogen's Saga.
         Boston, Houghton Mifflin, 1963.
    621. A Slave's Tale.
         Boston, Houghton Mifflin, 1965.

This is a stirring series about life in the violent Norway of the Vikings. The attention to historical detail is careful. Characters are presented realistically and developed through each book. An outstanding series centered around a little-written-about period.

HAYES, William D.

    622. Project: Genius.
         New York, Atheneum, 1962.
    623. Project: Scoop.
         New York, Atheneum, 1966.

Young Pete gets into various difficulties as he takes over the editorship of his school paper. He leans on spicy subjects and misquotes to boost interest in the paper. A very enjoyable series for Henry Reed and Homer Price fans.

HAYWOOD, Carolyn

    BETSY AND EDDIE SERIES

    624. "B" Is for Betsy.
         New York, Harcourt, 1939.
    625. Betsy and Billy.
         New York, Harcourt, 1941.
    626. Back to School with Betsy.
         New York, Harcourt, 1943.

HAYWOOD, Carolyn—continued

627. Betsy and the Boys.
   New York, Harcourt, 1945.
628. Little Eddie.
   New York, Morrow, 1947.
629. Eddie and the Fire Engine.
   New York, Morrow, 1949.
630. Betsy's Little Star.
   New York, Morrow, 1950.
631. Eddie and Gardenia.
   New York, Morrow, 1951.
632. Eddie's Pay Dirt.
   New York, Morrow, 1953.
633. Betsy and the Circus.
   New York, Morrow, 1954.
634. Eddie and His Big Deals.
   New York, Morrow, 1955.
635. Betsy's Busy Summer.
   New York, Morrow, 1956.
636. Eddie Makes Music.
   New York, Morrow, 1957.
637. Betsy's Winterhouse.
   New York, Morrow, 1958.
638. Eddie and Louella.
   New York, Morrow, 1959.
639. Annie Pat and Eddie.
   New York, Morrow, 1960.
640. Snowbound with Betsy.
   New York, Morrow, 1962.
641. Eddie's Green Thumb.
   New York, Morrow, 1964.
642. Eddie the Dogholder.
   New York, Morrow, 1966.
643. Betsy and Mr. Kilpatrick.
   New York, Morrow, 1967.
644. Ever-Ready Eddie.
   New York, Morrow, 1968.
645. Merry Christmas from Betsy.
   New York, Morrow, 1970.
646. Eddie's Happenings.
   New York, Morrow, 1971.

Here is another massive series that has spanned several generations with no apparent gap. Its popularity stems from the reality of characters and situa-

HAYWOOD, Carolyn—continued

tions that allow children to identify with them. The large print and pictures help make them easy to read. Through the years, Ms. Haywood has managed to retain a fresh approach that makes each story natural and lifelike. Can't miss with any of them.

    647. Here Comes the Bus.
          New York, Morrow, 1963.
    648. Taffy and Melissa Molasses.
          New York, Morrow, 1969.

This series is not as popular as the Betsy books, but it is still worthwhile, because the same fresh approach with children can be found here.

HEADLEY, Elizabeth (pseud.)
    See CAVANNA, Betty

HEIDE, Florence, and Sylvia VanClief

    SPOTLIGHT CLUB SERIES

    649. The Mystery of the Silver Tag. (Pilot Book)
          Chicago, Whitman, 1972.
    650. The Mystery of the Missing Suitcase. (Pilot Book)
          Chicago, Whitman, 1972.

This is a new mystery series put out by Whitman, intended for the reluctant reader. The plots are not strong, the characterizations are nil, but they might appeal, due to large type and easy-to-read format.

HENRY, Marguerite

    BEEBE FAMILY SERIES

    651. Misty of Chincoteague.
          New York, Rand McNally, 1947.
    652. Sea Star.
          New York, Rand McNally, 1949.
    653. Stormy, Misty's Foal.
          New York, Rand McNally, 1963.

This is an excellent series by Ms. Henry. She combines adventure, excitement, and a knowledge of horses in these stories of a family raising horses on Chincoteague Island. Wesley Dennis's fine illustrations enhance the appeal of the books.

HEUMAN, William

    654. City High Five.
        New York, Dodd, 1964.
    655. City High Champs.
        New York, Dodd, 1969.

Related book:

    656. Backcourt Man.
        New York, Dodd, 1960.

This series is about the activities of Mike Harrigan and Pedro Martinez, as they drive their basketball team to a city-wide victory. The related book concerns Mike's brother, Richie. Generally fast-moving sports action, the second book descends into moralizing about race relations, and so is not as well done as the other two books. Still, they will be popular with boys 10 to 14.

HORACE HIGBY SERIES

    657. Horace Higby and the Field Goal Formula.
        New York, Dodd, 1965.
    658. Horace Higby and the Scientific Pitch.
        New York, Dodd, 1968.
    659. Horace Higby, Coxswain of the Crew.
        New York, Dodd, 1971.

Horace Higby invades sports, using his scientific knowledge to give his team the advantage. Ridiculous but fun for sports-minded boys.

HICKS, Clifford

ALVIN FERNALD SERIES

    660. The Marvelous Inventions of Alvin Fernald.
        New York, Holt, 1960.
    661. Alvin's Secret Code.
        New York, Holt, 1963.
    662. Alvin Fernald, Foreign Trader.
        New York, Holt, 1966.
    663. Alvin Fernald, Mayor for a Day.
        New York, Holt, 1970.

Another set of hilarious books for boys. Alvin's adventures are absurd and ridiculous, but are presented with an air of reality that is most convincing.

HILDICK, E. W.

    664. The Secret Winners.
        New York, Crown, 1970.
    665. The Secret Spenders.
        New York, Crown, 1971.

This new series has excellent characterizations as well as intriguing plots. Both are humorous, although the second book ends with the resolution of a life and death situation. Still, they are cohesive and well written.

    BIRDY JONES SERIES

    666. Birdy Jones.
        New York, Stackpole, 1969.
    667. Birdy and the Group.
        New York, Stackpole, 1969.

This is a far-out series with the hero a high school lad who becomes a sensation whistling pop music. For those with zany senses of humor.

    668. Louie's Lot.
        New York, David White, 1968.
    669. Louie's SOS.
        New York, Doubleday, 1970.

Another of Hildick's stories with an unusual twist. This time the action surrounds a milkman in a small English town. The writing is witty, the action fast; the appeal will be to readers in grades 5 to 7.

HILL, Margaret

    670. Goal in the Sky.
        Boston, Little, 1953.
    671. Hostess in the Sky.
        Boston, Little, 1955.
    672. Senior Hostess.
        Boston, Little, 1958.

Another teenage career series, this one follows Beth Dean as she endeavors to become a stewardess. Mediocre fare.

    673. Really Miss Hillsbro.
        Boston, Little, 1960.
    674. The Extra-Special Room.
        Boston, Little, 1962.

HILL, Margaret—continued

Another teenage series by this author, this one is about a teacher. All right reading for girls in grades 7 to 9.

HODGES, C. Walter

    675. The Namesake.
        New York, Coward, 1964.
    676. The Marsh King.
        New York, Coward, 1967.

This compelling series about England during the reign of Alfred the Great concentrates on his efforts to drive the Danes out of his country. His story is paralleled by that of a young boy named Alfred. The characterizations are excellent, coverage of the period and historical accuracy far above the average. These books also have the added advantage of Mr. Hodges' own illustrations.

HODGES, Margaret

    JOSHUA COBB SERIES
    677. The Hatching of Joshua Cobb.
        New York, Farrar, 1967.
    678. The Making of Joshua Cobb.
        New York, Farrar, 1971.

This is an uneven series about the growing up of the boy Joshua Cobb. The first book is well done, but the second is stilted and contrived.

HONNESS, Elizabeth

    679. The Mystery at the Doll Hospital.
        Philadelphia, Lippincott, 1955.
    680. The Mystery in the Square Tower.
        Philadelphia, Lippincott, 1957.

Here is a mystery series for younger readers that has appealing characters in the Day children. The plots are somewhat improbable, but they are nonetheless highly readable. For those from 9 to 12.

    681. The Mystery of the Auction Trunk.
        Philadelphia, Lippincott, 1956.

HONNESS, Elizabeth—continued

    682. The Mystery of the Wooden Indian.
        Philadelphia, Lippincott, 1958.

Another mystery series by this author. This one should have the same appeal as the other. The main characters this time are the Holland children.

HORSEMAN, Elaine

    683. Hubble's Bubble.
        New York, Norton, 1964.
    684. The Hubbles' Treasure Hunt.
        New York, Norton, 1965.

The Hubble family becomes involved in magic when their scientific son, Alaric, discovers an ancient book of spells and puts it to use. Good fantasy-adventure for readers 9 to 12.

HOSFORD, Jessie

    685. An Awful Name to Live Up To.
        New York, Hawthorne, 1969.
    686. You Bet Your Boots, I Can.
        New York, Nelson, 1972.

A young girl living in Nebraska in 1901 has the admittedly awful name of Julia Ward Howe Hoffman. With a name like that she finds that people expect things of her. And she proceeds to live up to this expectation. She eventually goes off to a teaching assignment on her own, a relatively unusual decision for that time. A combination prairie adventure and young teen career-romance series, this will appeal to 12-year-olds on up.

HUGHES, Walter Llewellyn
    See WALTERS, Hugh, pseud.

HUNT, Mabel Leigh

    687. Stars for Cristy.
        Philadelphia, Lippincott, 1956.
    688. Cristy at Skippinghills.
        Philadelphia, Lippincott, 1958.

HUNT, Mabel Leigh—continued

Cristy Romano moves with her family from a city tenement to a small town. The plots, although relatively uneventful, give a good picture of day-to-day family life, and the difficulties of adjustment in such a situation. For ages 9 to 12.

ICENHOWER, Joseph

    MR. MURDOCK SERIES

    689. Mr. Midshipman Murdock and the Barbary Pirates.
          Philadelphia, Winston, 1956.
    690. Mr. Murdock Takes Command.
          Philadelphia, Winston, 1958.

These tales are action-packed, much in the tradition of the Hornblower series. In fact, Icenhower's books could be used as introductory reading for those a little too young to read Forester. Especially good for boys 11 to 14.

INGER, Nan, pseud. (Ostman, Nan Inger)

    691. Katie and Nan.
         Translated by Annabelle MacMillan
         New York, Harcourt, 1965.
    692. Katie and Nan Go to Sea.
         Translated by Annabelle MacMillan
         New York, Harcourt, 1966.

Two sisters living in an apartment building band together to make friends and foes alike in these warm family stories. In the second book, they go on a cruise with the rest of their family, causing havoc wherever they turn. Fun for readers 7 to 11.

INYART, Gene

    693. Jenny.
         New York, Watts, 1966.
    694. Orange October.
         New York, Watts, 1968.

Jenny faces several traumas: losing her play "jungle" next door and having a bad year in school. Both problems are nicely resolved. Good characterizations and realistic dialogue make this a natural for ages 9 to 12.

JACKSON, Caary Paul

BUD BAKER SERIES

695. Bud Plays Junior High Football.
    New York, Hastings, 1957.
696. Bud Plays Junior High Basketball.
    New York, Hastings, 1959.
697. Bud Baker, T Quarterback.
    New York, Hastings, 1960.
698. Bud Baker, Racing Swimmer.
    New York, Hastings, 1962.
699. Bud Plays Senior High Basketball.
    New York, Hastings, 1964.
700. Bud Baker, High School Pitcher.
    New York, Hastings, 1967.
701. Bud Baker, College Pitcher.
    New York, Hastings, 1970.

These are very well-done sports stories which contain a lot of factual information about the sports involved. Although they begin with Bud in junior high, the writing is simple and all but the last three would be of interest to boys 9 to 12.

JACKSON, Jacqueline

RICHARDS FAMILY SERIES

702. The Paleface Redskins.
    Boston, Little, 1958.
703. The Ghost Boat.
    Boston, Little, 1969.

Both books are well-written, fluffy mysteries that will be especially appealing to girls 9 to 12. They could be used with reluctant readers as well.

JACKSON, Jesse

CHARLEY MOSS SERIES

704. Call Me Charley.
    New York, Harper, 1945.
705. Anchor Man.
    New York, Harper, 1947.
706. Charley Starts from Scratch.
    New York, Harper, 1958.

JACKSON, Jesse—continued

These stories are about a Negro boy, Charley Moss, as he tries out for the Olympic team. Racial issues are mentioned but are not dealt with as realistically as in the Graham books.

JACOBS, Flora Gill

    707. The Doll House Mystery.
        New York, Coward, 1958.
    708. The Toyshop Mystery.
        New York, Coward, 1960.

Here is an easy-to-read mystery series, especially for girls who are interested in dolls. Not very long on plot, but enjoyable. For grades 3 to 5.

JANSSON, Tove

    MOOMIN TALES

    709. Moominsummer Madness.
        Translated by Thomas Warburton
            New York, Walck, 1961.
    710. Moominland Midwinter.
        Translated by Thomas Warburton
            New York, Walck, 1962.
    711. Tales from Moomin Valley.
        Translated by Thomas Warburton
            New York, Walck, 1964.
    712. Finn Family Moomintroll.
        Translated by Elizabeth Portch
            New York, Walck, 1965.
    713. The Exploits of Moominpappa.
        Translated by Thomas Warburton
            New York, Walck, 1966.
    714. Moominpappa at Sea.
        Translated by Kingsley Hart
            New York, Walck, 1967.
    715. Comet in Moominland.
        Translated by Elizabeth Portch
            New York, Walck, 1968.
    716. Moominvalley in November.
        Translated by Kingsley Hart
            New York, Walck, 1971.

JANSSON, Tove—continued

Several of these fantasies have won the Hans Christian Andersen Award in their native Sweden. Along with an innocent humor, the author's drawings of various Moomin creatures create a complete, gentle world to delight readers.

KENDALL, Carol

> MINNIPINS SERIES
> 717. The Gammage Cup.
> > New York, Harcourt, 1959.
> 718. The Whisper of Glocken.
> > New York, Harcourt, 1965.

This fantasy about the imaginary Minnipins is outstanding. Ms. Kendall comments with a wry, sophisticated humor on the various foibles of humanity through the use of her imaginary people. The humor is subtle and there are plays on words. They can be read on one level by 9 to 12 year olds, but older children would appreciate them as well.

> 719. The Other Side of the Tunnel.
> > New York, Abelard, 1957.
> 720. The Big Splash.
> > New York, Viking, 1960.

Ms. Kendall has created another well-written series about Huggins and his friends. Her usual lively writing, strong characterization, and use of suspense are in full force here. For readers 10 to 12.

KIDDELL, John

> 721. Euloowirree Walkabout.
> > New York, Chilton, 1968.
> 722. A Community of Men.
> > New York, Chilton, 1969.

These books are set in Australia, thus the difficult first title. Three boys find themselves responsible for an orphaned boys' home. They try to manage it themselves, but finally realize that they must compromise for the total welfare. The presentation of the situation is realistic, characters are well portrayed, but the Aussie dialect may prove somewhat hard to handle for young readers.

KINGMAN, Lee

    TEDDY TIBBETTS SERIES

    723. The Saturday Gang.
            New York, Doubleday, 1961.
    724. Private Eyes.
            New York, Doubleday, 1964.

These are lively, atmospheric mysteries featuring Teddy Tebbitts and the Saturday Gang. Both have interesting backgrounds, the first taking place during the filming of a TV series and the second featuring sailboating.

KJELGAARD, Jim

    JASE MASON SERIES

    725. A Nose for Trouble.
            New York, Holiday, 1949.
    726. Trailing Trouble.
            New York, Holiday, 1952.
    727. Wildlife Cameraman.
            New York, Holiday, 1957.
    728. Hidden Trail.
            New York, Holiday, 1962.

This series is done with Mr. Kjelgaard's usual finesse, although some of the colloquialisms used in the earlier books may seem dated to young readers today.

KLEBERGER, Ilse

    729. Grandmother Oma.
            Translated by Belinda McGill
                New York, Atheneum, 1964.
    730. Traveling with Oma.
            Translated by Belinda McGill
                New York, Atheneum, 1970.

An unpredictable grandmother leads her grandchildren into many wild adventures. Great fun, even in translation. For reader 9 to 12.

KRUSS, James

    PAULINE SERIES

    731. Pauline and the Prince in the Wind.
        Translated by Edelgard von Heydekamp Bruhl
        New York, Atheneum, 1966.
    732. Letters to Pauline.
        Translated by Edelgard von Heydekamp Bruhl
        New York, Atheneum, 1971.

Both books are well-written, although the episodic format may disturb some readers. Both are written as a series of letters in story form from the author to a little girl named Pauline. It would be better to present them to prospective readers as short stories.

LADD, Elizabeth

    MEG SERIES

    733. Meg of Heron's Neck.
        New York, Morrow, 1961.
    734. A Mystery for Meg.
        New York, Morrow, 1962.
    735. Meg's Mysterious Island.
        New York, Morrow, 1963.
    736. Meg and Melissa.
        New York, Morrow, 1964.
    737. Trouble on Heron's Neck.
        New York, Morrow, 1966.
    738. Treasure on Heron's Neck.
        New York, Morrow, 1967.

This is generally a good mystery series. The second offering is rather stilted and some of the characters tend toward caricature, but the others make acceptable fare for girls 9 to 12.

LAKLAN, Carli

    NANCY KIMBALL SERIES

    739. Nancy Kimball, Nurse's Aide. (Signal Books)
        New York, Doubleday, 1962.
    740. Nurse in Training. (Signal Books)
        New York, Doubleday, 1965.

LAKLAN, Carli—continued

    741. Second Year Nurse. (Signal Books)
        New York, Doubleday, 1966.

This is an acceptable career series dealing with the problems of nurse's training. The easy-to-read format and high interest should make it appropriate for use with reluctant readers. For ages 11 on up.

LAMBERT, Janet

    JORDON FAMILY SERIES
    742. Just Jennifer.
        New York, Dutton, 1945.
    743. Friday's Child.
        New York, Dutton, 1947.
    744. Confusion—by Cupid.
        New York, Dutton, 1950.
    745. A Dream for Susan.
        New York, Dutton, 1954.
    746. Love Taps Gently.
        New York, Dutton, 1955.
    747. A Song in Their Hearts.
        New York, Dutton, 1956.
    748. Myself and I.
        New York, Dutton, 1957.
    749. The Stars Hang High.
        New York, Dutton, 1960.
    750. Wedding Bells.
        New York, Dutton, 1961.
    751. A Bright Tomorrow.
        New York, Dutton, 1965.
    752. Here's Marny.
        New York, Dutton, 1969.

One of Ms. Lambert's usual sorties into family life and the problems of growing up. Generally well done, but the last entry is poorly handled.

    PATTY AND GINGER SERIES
    753. We're Going Steady.
        New York, Dutton, 1958.
    754. Boy Wanted.
        New York, Dutton, 1959.
    755. Spring Fever.
        New York, Dutton, 1960.

LAMBERT, Janet—continued

    756. Summer Madness.
        New York, Dutton, 1962.
    757. Extra Special.
        New York, Dutton, 1963.
    758. On Her Own.
        New York, Dutton, 1964.

Typical Lambert. For readers 10 to 14.

    SUGAR BRADLEY SERIES

    759. Sweet as Sugar.
        New York, Dutton, 1968.
    760. Hi, Neighbor.
        New York, Dutton, 1968.

Another Lambert series.

    PARRI MacDONALD SERIES

    761. Introducing Parri.
        New York, Dutton, 1962.
    762. That's My Girl.
        New York, Dutton, 1964.
    763. Stagestruck Parri.
        New York, Dutton, 1966.
    764. My Davy.
        New York, Dutton, 1968.

This series will be just as appealing to girls as Ms. Lambert's others.

    CAMPBELL FAMILY SERIES

    765. The Precious Days.
        New York, Dutton, 1957.
    766. For Each Other.
        New York, Dutton, 1959.
    767. Forever and Ever.
        New York, Dutton, 1961.
    768. Five's a Crowd.
        New York, Dutton, 1963.
    769. First of All.
        New York, Dutton, 1966.

This series is not as well done as the others. Her treatment of such subjects as political unrest in Haiti is insipid in the extreme. Not worth having.

LAMBERT, Janet—continued

CINDA HOLLISTER SERIES

770. Cinda.
 New York, Dutton, 1954.
771. Fly Away, Cinda.
 New York, Dutton, 1956.
772. Big Deal.
 New York, Dutton, 1958.
773. Triple Trouble.
 New York, Dutton, 1965.
774. Love to Spark.
 New York, Dutton, 1967.

Another disappointing series by Ms. Lambert. The treatment of teenage problems is again handled in a goody-goody fashion.

LAMPMAN, Evelyn

SHY STEGOSAURUS SERIES

775. The Shy Stegosaurus of Cricket Creek.
 New York, Doubleday, 1955.
776. The Shy Stegosaurus of Indian Springs.
 New York, Doubleday, 1962.

This engaging series about a shy dinosaur is a good bet for fantasy lovers. The second does lack some of the spontaneity of the first, but it is still enjoyable.

LANGTON, Jane

HALL CHILDREN SERIES

777. The Diamond in the Window.
 New York, Harper, 1962.
778. The Swing in the Summerhouse.
 New York, Harper, 1967.
779. The Astonishing Stereoscope.
 New York, Harper, 1971.

This series is a fascinating compendium of fantasy and adventure in a turn-of-the-century setting. A good choice for the reader who likes the unusual.

LANGTON, Jane—continued

    780. The Majesty of Grace.
           New York, Harper, 1961.
    781. The Boyhood of Grace Jones.
           New York, Harper, 1972.

Tomboy Grace Jones, living at the end of the Depression, envisions herself not as wife and mother but rather as Trueblue Tom, first mate on the ship "The Flying Cloud." Grace's desire to experience the excitement of boys will be familiar to many girls. The author tells Grace's story with humor and perception. Better than average fare for ages 9 to 12.

LATTIMORE, Eleanor

    LITTLE PEAR SERIES

    782. Little Pear.
           New York, Harcourt, 1931.
    783. Little Pear and His Friends.
           New York, Harcourt, 1934.
    784. Little Pear and the Rabbits.
           New York, Harcourt, 1956.
    785. More About Little Pear.
           New York, Morrow, 1971.

Ms. Lattimore's series about a young Chinese boy possesses her usual charm, quiet humor, and understanding. For reader 8 to 12.

LAUBER, Patricia

    CLARENCE SERIES

    786. Clarence the TV Dog. (Gateway Books)
           New York, Coward, 1955.
    787. Clarence Goes to Town. (Gateway Books)
           New York, Coward, 1957.
    788. Clarence Turns Sea Dog. (Gateway Books)
           New York, Coward, 1959.

This is an ordinary series featuring a TV-watching dog. It is pleasant enough reading, but nothing special. For ages 8 to 11.

LAURITZEN, Jonreed

    MARRINER FAMILY SERIES
    789. The Young Mustangers.
           Boston, Little, 1957.
    790. Treasure of the High Country.
           Boston, Little, 1959.
    791. The Glitter-Eyed Wouser.
           Boston, Little, 1960.

These stories present strong characterizations, suspense, and atmosphere. Unfortunately, the third entry does have a sometimes improbable plot.

LAWRENCE, Mildred

    792. Drums in My Heart.
           New York, Harcourt, 1964.
    793. Gateway to the Sun.
           New York, Harcourt, 1970.

Val Revel must cope with the broken engagement of her sister in one novel, and with unpleasant step-siblings on a visit to her divorced father in the other. As old-fashioned as the situations may sound, the author still takes advantage of today's teenage problems. Val must decide between a group of pot smokers who are quite attractive and her unpleasant step-family. Somewhat pat in her handling, Ms. Lawrence still has an entertaining way with words. For ages 11 to 14.

LAWSON, Patrick (pseud.)
    See EBY, Lois

LEE, Robert C.

    MICHAEL GLENN SERIES
    794. The Iron Arm of Michael Glenn.
           Boston, Little, 1965.
    795. The Day It Rained Forever.
           Boston, Little, 1968.

Light, fast-paced adventures similar to but better than the Danny Dunn stories. Especially good for boys in grades 4 to 6 and for reluctant readers.

LE GUIN, Ursula

    796. The Wizard of Earthsea.
        New York, Parnassus, 1968.
    797. The Tombs of Atuan.
        New York, Atheneum, 1971.
    798. The Farthest Shore.
        New York, Atheneum, 1972.

An outstanding series, nominally a fantasy, but the themes can be read straightforwardly or as symbols. Highly recommended. The second entry was a Newbery Honor Book.

L'ENGLE, Madeleine

    AUSTIN FAMILY SERIES

    799. The 24 Days Before Christmas.
        New York, Farrar, 1964.
    800. Meet the Austins.
        New York, Vanguard, 1960.
    801. The Moon by Night.
        New York, Vanguard, 1963.
    802. The Young Unicorns.
        New York, Farrar, 1968.

These family stories are told with warmth and humor. They are perceptively written, with natural dialogue and good characterizations. They will appeal to girls 10 to 12, or even older.

LENT, Henry

    803. Jet Pilot.
        New York, Macmillan, 1959.
    804. Jet Pilot Overseas.
        New York, Macmillan, 1959.

This is a career series aimed at boys. Along with covering the training period and assignment to a squadron in Spain of the hero, Dick Martin, these books furnish information on the life of a pilot which will be of interest to boy readers.

LEWIS, C. S.

NARNIA TALES

805. The Lion, the Witch, and the Wardrobe.
New York, Macmillan, 1950.
806. Prince Caspian.
New York, Macmillan, 1951.
807. The Voyage of the "Dawn Treader."
New York, Macmillan, 1952.
808. The Silver Chair.
New York, Macmillan, 1953.
809. The Horse and His Boy.
New York, Macmillan, 1954.
810. The Magician's Nephew.
New York, Macmillan, 1955.
811. The Last Battle.
New York, Macmillan, 1956.

Here is Lewis's classic tale of the three children who travel to the land of Narnia and help rescue it from the icy evil which encloses it. A parable that is readable on several levels, it can be given to anyone from age 9 on up.

LEWIS, Mary Christianna (pseud. Christianna Brand)

NURSE MATILDA SERIES

812. Nurse Matilda.
New York, Dutton, 1964.
813. Nurse Matilda Goes to Town.
New York, Dutton, 1967.

A marvelously funny series, this follows in the footsteps of Mary Poppins. Nurse Matilda turns her naughty charges' bad deeds quite neatly back upon themselves. Edward Ardizzone's period illustrations illuminate his cousin's books delightfully.

LEWITON, Mina

RACHEL SERIES

814. Rachel.
New York, Watts, 1954.
815. Rachel and Herman.
New York, Watts, 1957.

LEWITON, Mina—continued

Set in New York, these books explore family life and boy-girl friendships with humor and nostalgia. Both children are appealing. For the 8 to 12 set.

    HUMPHREY SERIES
        816. Especially Humphrey.
            New York, Delacorte, 1967.
        817. Humphrey on the Town.
            New York, Delacorte, 1971.

A lovable sheepdog and his mistress attract all kinds of odd friends. The gentle humor should appeal to readers from 8 to 11.

LIGHTNER, A. M.

        818. The Planet Poachers.
            New York, Putnam, 1965.
        819. The Space Ark.
            New York, Putnam, 1968.

Here is another science fiction series with a twist—the hero is a wildlife ranger whose specialty is preserving alien wildlife from poaching or extinction. Science fiction with an emphasis on conservation, this will be popular with readers 9 to 14.

LINDGREN, Astrid

    BILL BERGSON SERIES
        820. Bill Bergson, Master Detective.
            Translated by Florence Lamborn
            New York, Viking, 1952.
        821. Bill Bergson Lives Dangerously.
            Translated by Florence Lamborn
            New York, Viking, 1954.
        822. Bill Bergson and the White Rose Rescue
            Translated by Florence Lamborn
            New York, Viking, 1965.

This is a rollicking mystery series about boy detective Bill Bergson. For children 9 to 12. The Swedish setting provides unusual atmosphere.

LINDGREN, Astrid—continued

PIPPI LONGSTOCKING SERIES

823. Pippi Longstocking.
　　Translated by Florence Lamborn
　　　New York, Viking, 1950.
824. Pippi Goes on Board.
　　Translated by Florence Lamborn
　　　New York, Viking, 1957.
825. Pippi in the South Seas.
　　Translated by Gerry Bothmer
　　　New York, Viking, 1959.

An uproariously funny series about a terribly strong little girl. It will appeal to the anti-establishment element in everyone, for she lives alone with no one to tell her what to do and just enough money to make her independent. (Alone, that is, except for the horse she keeps in the house.) Truly a delight.

KATI SERIES

826. Kati in Italy.
　　No translator given
　　　New York, Grosset, 1961.
827. Kati in Paris.
　　No translator given
　　　New York, Grosset, 1961.

A Swedish girl finds romance on a trip to Italy. She marries, then moves to Paris for further adventures. Not on a par with Ms. Lindgren's other series.

EMIL SERIES

828. Emil in the Soup Tureen.
　　No translator given
　　　Chicago, Follett, 1963.
829. Emil's Pranks.
　　No translator given
　　　Chicago, Follett, 1971.

Emil follows in the footsteps of the author's Pippi Longstocking. He is full of fun and adventure but lacks the spontaneity of his female predecessor. For readers 9 to 12.

LINDQUIST, Jennie

830. The Golden Name Day.
　　　New York, Harper, 1955.

LINDQUIST, Jennie—continued

    831. The Little Silver House.
        New York, Harper, 1959.
    832. The Crystal Tree.
        New York, Harper, 1966.

This is a warm, friendly series about a little American girl who is sent to live with relatives in Sweden for a year. Characters are well drawn, including the little girl, who is quite unhappy at first, but who grows to love her new home.

LITTLE, Jean

    833. Mine for Keeps.
        Boston, Little, 1962.
    834. Spring Begins in March.
        Boston, Little, 1966.

These are well-handled stories about a handicapped girl and how she faces her problems. The stories, told with vigor, humor, and compassion, are good for mature 10 to 12 year olds.

    835. Look Through My Window.
        New York, Harper, 1970.
    836. Kate.
        New York, Harper, 1971.

These books feature excellent characterizations and a strong portrayal of family life. The friendship of two girls is realistically portrayed, showing both their sameness and their differences. The second book's exploration of Kate's Jewishness and what it means to her is sensitively done. Recommended for ages 10 and up.

LORD, BEMAN

    SPACESHIP SERIES
    837. The Day the Spaceship Landed.
        New York, Walck, 1967.
    838. The Spaceship Returns.
        New York, Walck, 1970.

This is a good science fiction series for boys 8 to 10. The size of the books should be encouraging for reluctant readers as well.

LYNCH, Patricia

BROGEEN SERIES
839. Brogeen and the Little Wind.
     New York, Roy, 1962.
840. Brogeen Follows the Magic Tune.
     New York, Macmillan, 1968.
841. Brogeen and the Bronze Lizard.
     New York, Macmillan, 1970.

These tales are set in Ireland and the chief character is a leprechaun. Told in the Irish dialect, they are filled with magic, mischief, humor, and human foibles. Something special for fantasy lovers.

MacALVAY, Nora

CATHIE STUART SERIES
842. Cathie Stuart.
     New York, Viking, 1957.
843. Cathie and the Paddy Boy.
     New York, Viking, 1962.

Here is a series of historical novels set in Scotland during the nineteenth century. They give a good picture of family life on a farm during those times.

McCORMICK, Wilfred

ROCKY McCUNE SERIES
844. Captive Coach.
     New York, McKay, 1955.
845. The Bigger Game.
     New York, McKay, 1958.
846. The Hot Corner.
     New York, McKay, 1958.
847. Proud Champions.
     New York, McKay, 1959.
848. Five Yards to Glory.
     New York, McKay, 1959.
849. Too Many Forwards.
     New York, McKay, 1960.
850. The Automatic Strike.
     New York, McKay, 1960.

McCORMICK, Wilfred—continued

    851. The Double Steal.
        New York, McKay, 1961.
    852. The Play for One.
        New York, McKay, 1961.
    853. The Five-Man Break.
        New York, McKay, 1962.
    854. Home Run Harvest.
        New York, McKay, 1962.
    855. The Phantom Shortstop.
        New York, McKay, 1963.
    856. The Two-One Attack.
        New York, McKay, 1963.
    857. The Long Pitcher.
        New York, Duell, 1964.
    858. Wild on the Bases.
        New York, Duell, 1965.
    859. No Place for Heroes.
        Indianapolis, Bobbs-Merrill, 1966.
    860. Incomplete Pitcher.
        Indianapolis, Bobbs-Merrill, 1967.

This is an extensive sports series, perhaps too much so. The quality of writing is mediocre, the characterizations trite. What is worse, many characters with different names seem to be mere repetitions of those in past books. Perhaps a few for reluctant readers would be all right, but there are other sports writers for boys with much better quality output.

    861. First and Ten.
        New York, Speller, 1962.
    862. The Starmaker.
        New York, Speller, 1963.

Once more, the quality of this series is not up to that of the better fictional sports writers.

    BRONC BURNETT SERIES

    863. The Three-Two Pitch.
        New York, Putnam, 1948.
    864. Legion Tourney.
        New York, Putnam, 1948.
    865. Fielder's Choice.
        New York, Putnam, 1949.

McCORMICK, Wilfred—continued

866. Flying Tackle.
    New York, Putnam, 1949.
867. Rambling Halfback.
    New York, Putnam, 1950.
868. Bases Loaded.
    New York, Putnam, 1950.
869. Grand Slam Homer.
    New York, Putnam, 1951.
870. Quick Kid.
    New York, Putnam, 1951.
871. Eagle Scout.
    New York, Putnam, 1952.
872. The Big Ninth.
    New York, Grosset, 1958.
873. The Last Put-Out.
    New York, Putnam, 1960.
874. One O'Clock Hitter.
    New York, Grosset, 1960.
875. Stranger in the Backfield.
    New York, McKay, 1960.
876. The Bluffer.
    New York, McKay, 1961.
877. Man in Motion.
    New York, McKay, 1961.
878. Rebel with a Glove.
    New York, McKay, 1962.
879. Too Late to Quit.
    New York, McKay, 1962.
880. Once a Slugger.
    New York, McKay, 1963.
881. Rough Stuff.
    New York, McKay, 1963.
882. The Right-End Option.
    New York, McKay, 1964.
883. The Throwaway Catcher.
    New York, McKay, 1964.
884. The Go-Ahead Runner.
    New York, McKay, 1965.
885. Seven in Front.
    New York, McKay, 1965.
886. Tall at the Plate.
    Indianapolis, Bobbs-Merrill, 1966.

McCORMICK, Wilfred—continued

Just as with the Rocky McCune series, this one suffers from too much of a not-so-good thing. Only for die-hard sports fans.

MacGREGOR, Ellen

> MISS PICKERELL SERIES
> Those preceded by a dash are written with Dora Pantell.

887. Miss Pickerell Goes to Mars.
New York, McGraw, 1951.
888. Miss Pickerell and the Geiger Counter.
New York, McGraw, 1953.
889. Miss Pickerell Goes Undersea.
New York, McGraw, 1953.
890. Miss Pickerell Goes to the Arctic.
New York, Whittlesey House, 1954.
−891. Miss Pickerell on the Moon.
New York, McGraw, 1965.
−892. Miss Pickerell Goes on a Dig.
New York, McGraw, 1966.
−893. Miss Pickerell Harvests the Sea.
New York, McGraw, 1968.
−894. Miss Pickerell and the Weather Satellite.
New York, McGraw, 1970.

The quality of this series divides evenly. The first half are great fun, some science fiction, but more science fact introduced in a humorous form. Unfortunately, the new co-author has not done well by Ms. MacGregor, for the quality of the series really degenerates. Plots, characters, and dialogue are stilted and unconvincing.

McILVAINE, Jane

> CAMMIE SERIES

895. Cammie's Choice.
Indianapolis, Bobbs-Merrill, 1961.
896. Cammie's Challenge.
Indianapolis, Bobbs-Merrill, 1962.
897. Cammie's Cousin.
Indianapolis, Bobbs-Merrill, 1963.

These are adequate girls' stories about Camilla Moore. The second one, which is about horses, will be especially appealing to girls 9 to 12.

McLEAN, Allan Campbell

  898. Storm Over Skye.
    New York, Harcourt, 1956.
  899. Master of Morgana.
    New York, Harcourt, 1959.
  900. The Gates of Eden.
    New York, Harcourt, 1962.

Set on the island of Skye in the Scottish Hebrides, these adventure-mysteries have an unusual background as well as tightknit plots. The first two books are mysteries, but the third is a tribute to the island.

  901. Ribbon of Fire.
    New York, Harcourt, 1962.
  902. A Sound of Trumpets.
    New York, Harcourt, 1966.

These are well-paced adventures, again set in Scotland. The hero is Alasdair Stewart. There is a certain amount of violence in this series, but nothing that should be too upsetting to readers 11 to 14.

McNEILL, Janet

  903. The Battle of St. George Without.
    Boston, Little, 1966.
  904. Goodbye, Dove Square.
    Boston, Little, 1969.

These are excellent books set in present-day England. The characters are well drawn and show resilience and humor in the face of their problems. The second book is an especially terrifying adventure that might be better suited to more mature readers.

MANN, Peggy

  CARLOS SERIES
  905. The Street of the Flower Boxes.
    New York, Coward, 1966.
  906. The Clubhouse.
    New York, Coward, 1969.
  907. When Carlos Closed the Street.
    New York, Coward, 1969.

MANN, Peggy—continued

    908. How Juan Got Home.
        New York, Coward, 1972.

These stories about Carlos and his friends with various racial and ethnic backgrounds are realistically told, with natural plots evolving from city life—the need for play streets, the unhappiness of a newly-emigrated boy. For readers from 8 to 11.

MANTLE, Winifred

    909. The Hiding Place.
        New York, Holt, 1963.
    910. Tinker's Castle.
        New York, Holt, 1964.
    911. The Question of the Painted Cave.
        New York, Holt, 1966.
    912. The Penderel Puzzle.
        New York, Holt, 1966.

Well-written mysteries involving the Lester and Westcott children. This series has action and humor for both boys and girls 9 to 12.

MASON, Miriam

    CAROLINE SERIES

    913. Caroline and Her Kettle Named Maud.
        New York, Macmillan, 1951.
    914. Caroline and the Seven Little Words.
        New York, Macmillan, 1967.

This series, about a little girl in pioneer days, is best suited to the 8 to 10 age level. It is adequate, but nothing more.

MASTERS, Kelly (pseud. Zachary Ball)

    JASE LANDERS SERIES

    915. Bristle Face.
        New York, Holiday, 1962.
    916. Sputters.
        New York, Holiday, 1963.

MASTERS, Kelly—continued

These stories of a backwoods boy's adventures with animals are lively, amusing, full of colorful characters and regional speech. Especially recommended for boys 9 to 12.

JOE PANTHER SERIES

917. Swamp Chief.
New York, Holiday, 1952.
918. Skin Diver.
New York, Holiday, 1956.
919. Salvage Diver.
New York, Holiday, 1961.
920. Sky Diver.
New York, Holiday, 1967.

This is a good series about Indian Joe Panther and his work as a deep sea diver and salvager. Good for career-seekers.

MAULE, Tex

JIM BEATTY SERIES

921. The Shortstop.
New York, McKay, 1962.
922. Beatty of the Yankees.
New York, McKay, 1963.
923. The Last Out.
New York, McKay, 1964.

A good series for boys interested in professional baseball, this one shows the training and problems of player Jim Beatty. For more mature readers.

BRAD THOMAS SERIES

924. The Rookie.
New York, McKay, 1961.
925. The Quarterback.
New York, McKay, 1962.
926. Championship Quarterback.
New York, McKay, 1963.
927. The Receiver.
New York, McKay, 1968.

MAULE, Tex—continued

>Related to series:
>928. The Linebacker.
>>New York, McKay, 1965.
>929. The Corner Back.
>>New York, McKay, 1967.

Another convincing series for older boys about the life of a professional football player. Well-done, fast-moving stories.

MEANS, Florence

>930. Knock at the Door, Emmy.
>>Boston, Houghton Mifflin, 1956.
>931. Emmy and the Blue Door.
>>Boston, Houghton Mifflin, 1959.

Emmy Lou Lane, daughter of a migrant worker, wins a scholarship to college. She becomes a social worker in Mexico and is involved in a romance there. An early treatment of some of the problems encountered by migrant workers, this series still stands up well today. Recommended for readers 11 to 14.

MEYER, Franklyn

>932. Me and Caleb.
>>Chicago, Follett, 1962.
>933. Me and Caleb Again.
>>Chicago, Follett, 1969.

The first book of this series is far superior to the second, as it explores the relationship between brothers. Meyer's dialogue is natural and realistic, and the plot is funny, sad, and full of adventure. The second book, however, shows some discrepancy in that the age difference between the characters is less than in the first book, the name of their teacher changes inexplicably, and the characterizations seem to have gone down the drain.

MIRSKY, Reba

>NOMUSA SERIES
>
>934. Thirty-one Brothers and Sisters.
>>Chicago, Follett, 1952.

MIRSKY, Reba—continued

    935. Seven Grandmothers.
        Chicago, Follett, 1955.
    936. Nomusa and the New Magic.
        Chicago, Follett, 1962.

These are outstanding stories about a young Zulu girl. Life in the South African Kraal is presented in detail as she grows up and leaves to become a nurse. The theme in the last volume may be too advanced except for mature readers.

MOLARSKY, Osmond

    937. Song of the Empty Bottles
        New York, Walck, 1968.
    938. Song of the Smoggy Stars.
        New York, Walck, 1972.

Thaddeus, a young Negro boy, collects empty bottles to earn a much-longed-for guitar. His family and neighbors find the songs he composes on his guitar to be unusually meaningful. In the second book he goes on a camping trip, which makes him aware of the pollution in his city. He then decides to use his guitar, the only thing he has, to fight this pollution. Both stories are sensitively told with a realistic portrayal of the feelings of this young boy. The second book skirts the danger of climbing on the anti-pollution bandwagon. The only thing missing from the second book are Tom Feelings' soft-hued illustrations. For ages 6 to 10.

MONTGOMERY, Rutherford

    GOLDEN STALLION SERIES

    939. The Capture of the Golden Stallion.
        Boston, Little, 1951.
    940. The Golden Stallion's Revenge.
        Boston, Little, 1953.
    941. The Golden Stallion to the Rescue.
        Boston, Little, 1954.
    942. The Golden Stallion and the Wolf Dog.
        Boston, Little, 1958.
    943. The Golden Stallion's Victory.
        Boston, Little, 1958.

MONTGOMERY, Rutherford—continued

> 944. The Golden Stallion's Adventure at Redstone.
> Boston, Little, 1959.
> 945. The Golden Stallion and the Mysterious Feud.
> Boston, Little, 1967.

These horse stories, much along the line of Walter Farley's, are aimed at a slightly higher age group, from grades 7 and up. The plots and characterizations are trite, and unless they are to be used to gain the interest of reluctant readers, there is no real necessity for having them in a collection.

KENT BARSTOW SERIES

> 946. Kent Barstow, Special Agent.
> New York, Duell, 1958.
> 947. Missile Away.
> New York, Duell, 1959.
> 948. Mission Intruder.
> New York, Duell, 1960.
> 949. Kent Barstow, Spaceman.
> New York, Duell, 1961.
> 950. Kent Barstow and the Commando Flight.
> New York, Duell, 1963.
> 951. Kent Barstow on a B-70 Mission.
> New York, Duell, 1964.
> 952. Kent Barstow Aboard the Dyna Soar.
> New York, Duell, 1964.

Kent Barstow is an Intelligence Officer in the Air Force. His assignments include testing jet planes and catching spies. The quality of writing is not high, but these might be used with reluctant readers.

MOON, Sheila

MARIS SERIES

> 953. Knee Deep in Thunder.
> New York, Atheneum, 1967.
> 954. Hunt Down the Prize.
> New York, Atheneum, 1971.

An excellent series that combines adventure with symbolism, with strong characterizations. For the reader who likes something extra special.

MOSKIN, Marietta

    955. The Best Birthday Party.
          New York, John Day, 1964.
    956. With an Open Hand.
          New York, John Day, 1967.

This series follows the adventures of young Jennie growing up in a small New England town. All right fare for readers 9 to 12.

MOWAT, Farley

    957. Lost in the Barrens.
          Boston, Little, 1956.
    958. The Curse of the Viking Grave.
          Boston, Little, 1966.

These are adventure stories set in Canada. The first book, detailing survival in the wilds, is engrossing and more plausible than the second book. Nonetheless, they will both appeal to adventure story fans.

MUSGRAVE, Sarah

    959. Oh, Sarah.
          New York, Farrar, 1953.
    960. Sarah Hastings.
          New York, Farrar, 1960.

For the 12 to 16 age group, this series deals with a minister's only child who rebels against her upbringing. She becomes involved with volunteer activities during World War I. The appeal of this series is somewhat limited due to the old-fashioned morals it encompasses. Not necessary for today's teenagers.

NANKIVELL, Joice

    CHRISTOPHILOS SERIES
    961. Tales of Christophilos.
          Boston, Houghton Mifflin, 1954.
    962. Again Christophilos.
          Boston, Houghton Mifflin, 1959.

These stories are about the life, customs, and beliefs of people in a small town in Greece. Each chapter is a small tale of a different individual in the village, as seen through the eyes of Christophilos. Good for reading aloud, grades 3 to 6.

NASH, Mary

    MRS. COVERLET OR PERSEVER FAMILY SERIES

    963. While Mrs. Coverlet Was Away.
          Boston, Little, 1958.
    964. Mrs. Coverlet's Magicians.
          Boston, Little, 1961.
    965. Mrs. Coverlet's Detectives.
          Boston, Little, 1965.

Here is an amusing series about the Persever children and their adventures when their housekeeper is away. Appealing to children from 8 to 12.

NEUFELD, John

    966. Edgar Allen.
          New York, Phillips, 1968.
    967. Lisa Bright and Dark.
          New York, Phillips, 1970.

A white minister and his family decide to adopt a small black child. Eventually the minister gives in to community and family pressure and gives the child back. The next book finds a friend of Mary Nell succumbing to insanity. Mary Nell and some of her friends are the only ones who recognize this, and try, through group therapy sessions, to help her. Both novels are excellent. They have also gained a reputation with young readers as being straightforward and realistic in their treatment of these two hot subjects. A must for any collection.

NEWELL, Hope

    MARY ELLIS SERIES

    968. A Cap for Mary Ellis.
          New York, Harper, 1953.
    969. Mary Ellis, Student Nurse.
          New York, Harper, 1958.

Two books about a Negro girl who studies to become a nurse. The treatment of Negroes is sympathetic, but not very realistic. Many of the characters are stereotyped, rather like a Sue Barton book whose heroine just happens to be black.

NICOLE, Christopher, pseud. (York, Andrew)

    970. Operation Destruct.
          New York, Holt, 1969.
    971. Operation Manhunt.
          New York, Holt, 1970.
    972. Operation Neptune.
          New York, Holt, 1972.

Intended as spoofs of spy adventure stories, these books fail miserably to produce anything witty, satirical, or even interesting. The dialogue is dull, the plots are slow-moving and implausible, and the characterizations are ridiculous.

NORTON, Alice Mary (pseud. Andre Norton)

    KRIP VORLUND SERIES

    973. Moon of Three Rings.
          New York, Viking, 1966.
    974. Exiles of the Stars.
          New York, Viking, 1971.

The newest in a long series of series by Ms. Norton, this is as topnotch as the others. However, it may be better for more mature readers.

    HOSTEEN STORM SERIES

    975. Beast Master.
          New York, Harcourt, 1959.
    976. Lord of Thunder.
          New York, Harcourt, 1962.

One of the best of Ms. Norton's science fiction series.

    977. The Zero Stone.
          New York, Viking, 1968.
    978. Uncharted Stars.
          New York, Viking, 1969.

Another exciting science-fiction duo.

    TRAVIS FOX SERIES

    979. Galactic Derelict.
          Cleveland, World, 1959.
    980. The Defiant Agents.
          Cleveland, World, 1962.

More intriguing science fiction stories for mature readers.

NORTON, Alice Mary—continued

ROSS MURDOCK SERIES
981. The Time Traders.
   Cleveland, World, 1958.
982. Key Out of Time.
   Cleveland, World, 1963.

Another imaginative, well-written series of science fiction.

SHANN LANTEE SERIES
983. Storm Over Warlock.
   Cleveland, World, 1960.
984. Ordeal in Otherwhere.
   Cleveland, World, 1964.

The first volume of this series is well plotted, but the second seems too far-fetched and the characters too one-dimensional.

985. The Stars Are Ours.
   Cleveland, World, 1954.
986. Star Born.
   Cleveland, World, 1957.

An early science fiction series, still intriguing for the 9 to 12 age group.

AYYAR SERIES
987. Judgement on Janus.
   New York, Harcourt, 1963.
988. Victory on Janus.
   New York, Harcourt, 1966.

Another good science-fiction series for 9 to 12 year olds.

WITCH WORLD SERIES
989. Witch World.
   New York, Ace Books, 1963.
990. Web of the Witch World.
   New York, Ace Books, 1964.
991. Three Against the Witch World.
   New York, Ace Books, 1965.
992. Warlock of the Witch World.
   New York, Ace Books, 1967.
993. Sorceress of the Witch World.
   New York, Ace Books, 1968.

This is a good paperback series, especially for teenagers.

NORTON, Alice Mary—continued

    DREW RENNIE SERIES
    994. Ride Proud, Rebel.
        Cleveland, World, 1961.
    995. Rebel Spurs.
        Cleveland, World, 1962.

This series marks a departure into the historical realm for Ms. Norton, who here follows the adventures of young Drew Rennie during and after the Civil War. Action-filled, a very good way to impart some historical knowledge to boys.

NORTON, Andre (pseud.)
    See NORTON, Alice Mary

NORTON, Mary

    BORROWERS SERIES
    996. The Borrowers.
        New York, Harcourt, 1952.
    997. The Borrowers Afield.
        New York, Harcourt, 1955.
    998. The Borrowers Afloat.
        New York, Harcourt, 1959.
    999. The Borrowers Aloft.
        New York, Harcourt, 1961.
    1000. Poor Stainless.
        New York, Harcourt, 1971.

Here is an outstanding series of delightful fantasies about tiny people who live alongside people by "borrowing" from them. Ms. Norton creates a complete world that seems just as real as ours. For children of all ages. Wonderful illustrations by Beth and Joe Krush enhance the attractiveness of the series.

O'CONNOR, Patrick (pseud.)
    See WIBBERLY, Leonard

OFFIT, Sydney

    1001. Cadet Quarterback.
        New York, St. Martin's, 1961.

OFFIT, Sydney—continued

    1002. Cadet Command.
        New York, St. Martin's, 1962.
    1003. Cadet Attack.
        New York, St. Martin's, 1964.

While the plots are far from original, still, Bruce Newell's adventures as a cadet are fun to read and can be used with service-career-oriented boys.

OGILVIE, Elizabeth

    1004. Blueberry Summer.
        New York, McGraw, 1956.
    1005. The Fabulous Year.
        New York, McGraw, 1958.

This series follows chubby Cass into young womanhood. Not a good offering in this line: the dialogue is artificial, the characterizations tepid. The problems of the chubby girl growing up are better handled in Orgel's *Next Door to Xanadu*.

ORGEL, Doris

    CINDY SERIES

    1006. Cindy's Snowdrops.
        New York, Knopf, 1966.
    1007. Cindy's Sad and Happy Tree.
        New York, Knopf, 1967.

These are sensitive books whose format would seem to indicate an 8 to 10 age group, but the subject matter, which is almost impressionistic, is really for an older, more aware age group. Ati Forberg's soft, gentle illustrations lend tremendously to the mood of the stories, especially in the second book, where the drawings and text are on beige paper.

OSTMAN, Nan Inger
    See INGER, Nan, pseud.

OTERDAHL, Jeanna

    1008. April Adventure.
        Translated by Annabelle MacMillan
        New York, Harcourt, 1962.

OTERDAHL, Jeanna—continued

    1009. Tina and the Latchkey Child.
           Translated by Annabelle MacMillan
           New York, Harcourt, 1963.
    1010. Island Summer.
           Translated by Annabelle MacMillan
           New York, Harcourt, 1964.

These stories follow the friendship of two Norwegian girls. Their everyday adventures and pleasures will be most enjoyable for grades 3 to 5.

OTTLEY, Reginald

    1011. Boy Alone.
           New York, Harcourt, 1966.
    1012. The Roan Colt.
           New York, Harcourt, 1967.
    1013. Rain Comes to Yamboorah.
           New York, Harcourt, 1967.

These are compelling stories about a boy's life in the Australian bush country. Plots are exciting and the atmosphere and mood of the country are accurately captured. Dialogue is fresh and the Australian vernacular is kept to an understandable minimum.

PALLAS, Norvin

    1014. The Secret of Thunder Mountain.
           New York, Washburn, 1951.
    1015. The Locked Safe Mystery.
           New York, Washburn, 1954.
    1016. The Star Reporter Mystery.
           New York, Washburn, 1955.
    1017. The Singing Trees Mystery.
           New York, Washburn, 1956.
    1018. The Empty House Mystery.
           New York, Washburn, 1957.
    1019. The Counterfeit Mystery.
           New York, Washburn, 1958.
    1020. The Scarecrow Mystery.
           New York, Washburn, 1960.

PALLAS, Norvin—continued

    1021. The Big Cat Mystery.
           New York, Washburn, 1961.
    1022. The Missing Witness Mystery.
           New York, Washburn, 1962.
    1023. The Baseball Mystery.
           New York, Washburn, 1963.
    1024. The Mystery of Rainbow Gulch.
           New York, Washburn, 1964.
    1025. The Abandoned Mine Mystery.
           New York, Washburn, 1965.
    1026. The "S.S. Shamrock" Mystery.
           New York, Washburn, 1966.
    1027. The Greenhouse Mystery.
           New York, Washburn, 1967.

Young Ted Wilford is a newspaper reporter with a penchant for getting himself involved in mysteries. O.K. for readers 9 to 12.

PANTELL, Dora
    See MacGREGOR, Ellen

PARISH, Peggy

    1028. Key to the Treasure.
           New York, Macmillan, 1967.
    1029. Clues in the Woods.
           New York, Macmillan, 1968.
    1030. Haunted House.
           New York, Macmillan, 1971.

Generally a good series of mysteries involving the three children in the Roberts family. Simple enough for the 8 to 10 age group. The newest offering is weaker in plot than the others.

PATCHETT, Mary

    BRUMBY SERIES

    1031. Brumby, the Wild White Stallion.
           Indianapolis, Bobbs-Merrill, 1959.

PATCHETT, Mary—continued

    1032. Brumby, Come Home.
           Indianapolis, Bobbs-Merrill, 1962.

Another series of horse stories fine for girls 9 to 12, but nothing extraordinary.

PEASE, Howard

    TOD MORAN MYSTERY SERIES

    1033. The Tattooed Man.
           New York, Doubleday, 1926.
    1034. The Jinx Ship.
           New York, Doubleday, 1927.
    1035. Shanghai Passage.
           New York, Doubleday, 1929.
    1036. The Ship Without a Crew.
           New York, Doubleday, 1934.
    1037. Hurricane Weather.
           New York, Doubleday, 1936.
    1038. Foghorn.
           New York, Doubleday, 1937.
    1039. Highroad to Adventure.
           New York, Doubleday, 1939.
    1040. The Black Tanker.
           New York, Doubleday, 1941.
    1041. Night Boat.
           New York, Doubleday, 1942.
    1042. Heart of Danger.
           New York, Doubleday, 1946.
    1043. Wind in the Rigging.
           New York, Doubleday, 1953.
    1044. Captain of the "Araby."
           New York, Doubleday, 1953.
    1045. Mystery on Telegraph Hill.
           New York, Doubleday, 1961.

This is a generally good, if somewhat old-fashioned series. Some of the older books are still in print, but the colloquialisms and writing style of 30 years ago may put off some young readers. Better to stick with the more recent ones, although there are better modern mystery writers for boys, such as Scott Corbett.

PETERSON, Hans

MAGNUS SERIES

1046. Magnus and the Squirrel.
Translated by Madeleine Hamilton
New York, Viking, 1959.
1047. Magnus and the Wagon Horse.
Translated by Marianne Turner
New York, Pantheon, 1966.
1048. Magnus in the Harbor.
Translated by Marianne Turner
New York, Pantheon, 1966.
1049. Magnus in Danger.
Translated by Marianne Turner
New York, Pantheon, 1967.
1050. Magnus and the Ship's Mascot.
Translated by Marianne Turner
New York, Pantheon, 1967.

These stories with a Swedish background follow the adventures of young Magnus. There is much action in his everyday life. The characters are well developed, and the translation generally good. An appealing series for the younger reader, 8 to 11.

PETERSON, John

1051. The Secret Hide-Out.
New York, Four Winds, 1966.
1052. Enemies of the Secret Hide-Out.
New York, Four Winds, 1966.

These are short, easy-to-read stories of the adventures of three boys who form a club. Their adventures are common to many boys in similar situations, and so these stories should prove popular. For ages 8 to 11.

PEYTON, K. M.

FLAMBARDS SERIES

1053. Flambards.
Cleveland, World, 1967.
1054. The Edge of the Cloud.
Cleveland, World, 1969.

PEYTON, K. M.—continued

    1055. Flambards in Summer.
          Cleveland, World, 1969.

This series is for mature readers and teenagers. It concerns various characters who live in the English town of Flambards. A combination of melodrama and soap opera, yet handled with style and flair, this series will be especially popular with girls. The first and third members of the series were Notable Books.

    1056. Pennington's Last Term.
          New York, Crowell, 1971.
    1057. The Beethoven Medal.
          New York, Crowell, 1972.

A vivid story of a young boy who fights the Establishment, endangering his blooming romance and possible career as a concert pianist. For the teenage reader.

PHILBROOK, Clem

    OLLIE SERIES
    1058. Ollie's Team and the Baseball Computer.
          New York, Hastings, 1967.
    1059. Ollie's Team and the Football Computer.
          New York, Hastings, 1968.
    1060. Ollie's Team and the Basketball Computer.
          New York, Hastings, 1969.
    1061. Ollie's Team Plays Biddy Baseball.
          New York, Hastings, 1970.
    1062. Ollie, the Backward Forward.
          New York, Hastings, 1970.
    1063. Ollie's Team and the Alley Cats.
          New York, Hastings, 1971.
    1064. Ollie's Team and the 200 Pound Problem.
          New York, Hastings, 1972.

Sports stories in the humorous vein of the Horace Higby series, these will be enjoyed by boys 9 to 12.

PHIPSON, Joan

    BARKER FAMILY SERIES

    1065. Good Luck to the Rider.
           New York, Harcourt, 1968.
    1066. The Family Conspiracy.
           New York, Harcourt, 1964.
    1067. Threat to the Barkers.
           New York, Harcourt, 1965.

An excellent series about an Australian family. Each member of the family is an individual, the dialogue is flavorful, and the atmosphere is exciting.

PINKERTON, Kathrene

    1068. Hidden Harbor.
           New York, Harcourt, 1951.
    1069. Year of Enchantment.
           New York, Harcourt, 1957.

Set in Alaska at the turn of the century, these novels about the Baird family are well done. The depiction of life in the wild, especially the segments on salmon fishing, are vivid. For those who like the Margaret Bell books.

PITKIN, Dorothy

    KIT HARRIS SERIES

    1070. The Grass Was That High.
           New York, Pantheon, 1959.
    1071. Wiser Than Winter.
           New York, Pantheon, 1960.

An excellent series about adolescent Kit Harris. Her problems are sensitively handled. Girls should identify with her. For more mature readers.

PLATT, Kin

    1072. The Blue Man.
           New York, Chilton, 1961.
    1073. Sinbad and Me.
           New York, Chilton, 1966.

PLATT, Kin—continued

>1074. The Mystery of the Witch Who Wouldn't.
>New York, Chilton, 1969.

This is an unusually well-done series with rather odd plots. The first book is science fiction with a suitably exaggerated plot. The second book concerns witchcraft, while the third book is a mystery and won The Mystery Writers' of America Award. Unusual reading for grades 5 through 9.

PLOWMAN, Stephanie

>1075. Three Lives for the Czar.
>Boston, Houghton Mifflin, 1969.
>1076. My Kingdom for a Grave.
>Boston, Houghton Mifflin, 1971.

An excellent new series set in Russia at the time of the czars. Historical background is fascinating and the series is adventuresome enough to interest mature readers of both sexes.

POLLAND, Madeleine

>1077. The Queen's Blessing.
>New York, Holt, 1964.
>1078. To Kill a King.
>New York, Holt, 1970.

Ms. Polland is an exceptional writer of historical fiction. The first book of this series is one of her best. Set in Scotland during the eleventh century, these stories detail the efforts of young Merca to kill the Scottish king. She meets Queen Margaret (later made a saint) and changes her mind. Characterizations are excellent, the plot is strong, background details are convincing. Unfortunately, the second novel finds too much interference in a secondary love story, and so the main plot loses some of its strength. Still, better than most. For grades 7 to 9.

POTTER, Bronson

>1079. Isfendiar and the Wild Donkeys.
>New York, Atheneum, 1967.
>1080. Isfendiar and the Bears of Mazandaran.
>New York, Atheneum, 1969.

POTTER, Bronson—continued

This series has an unusual setting in present-day Iran. Young Isfendiar must suffer many trials and have his heroism tested before he reaches manhood. Good stories with limited appeal for ages 8 through 12.

PRICE, Willard

    1081. Amazon Adventure.
          New York, John Day, 1949.
    1082. South Sea Adventure.
          New York, John Day, 1952.
    1083. Underwater Adventure.
          New York, John Day, 1954.
    1084. Volcano Adventure.
          New York, John Day, 1956.
    1085. Whale Adventure.
          New York, John Day, 1960.
    1086. African Adventure.
          New York, John Day, 1963.
    1087. Elephant Adventure.
          New York, John Day, 1964.
    1088. Safari Adventure.
          New York, John Day, 1966.
    1089. Lion Adventure.
          New York, John Day, 1967.
    1090. Gorilla Adventure.
          New York, John Day, 1969.
    1091. Diving Adventure.
          New York, John Day, 1970.
    1092. Crocodile Adventure.
          New York, John Day, announced.

Hal and Roger Hunt find themselves (obviously) in a lot of adventures. While the plots are often improbable, action is fast moving, and the books have the added benefit of containing some scientific information on each exploit, i.e., on volcanoes, animal life, life beneath the sea, etc. For readers 10 to 14.

PROYSEN, Alf

    MRS. PEPPERPOT SERIES
    1093. Little Old Mrs. Pepperpot.
          Translated by Marianne Helweg
          New York, McDowell, 1959.

PROYSEN, Alf—continued

    1094. Mrs. Pepperpot Again.
        Translated by Marianne Helweg
           New York, McDowell, 1960.
    1095. Mrs. Pepperpot to the Rescue.
        Translated by Marianne Helweg
           New York, Pantheon, 1963.
    1096. Mrs. Pepperpot in the Magic Wood.
        Translated by Marianne Helweg
           New York, Pantheon, 1968.
    1097. Mrs. Pepperpot's Outing.
        Translated by Marianne Helweg
           New York, Pantheon, 1971.

Each volume contains not one but several stories about the feisty Mrs. Pepperpot, so called because she can become as tiny as a pepperpot. Much fun for kids from 8 on up, with piquant drawings by Bjorn Berg.

REEDER, Red

    1098. West Point Plebe.
        New York, Duell, 1955.
    1099. West Point Yearling.
        New York, Duell, 1956.
    1100. West Point Second Classman.
        New York, Duell, 1957.
    1101. West Point First Classman.
        New York, Duell, 1958.
    1102. Second Lieutenant Clint Lane.
        New York, Duell, 1960.
    1103. Clint Lane in Korea.
        New York, Duell, 1961.

Since Col. Reeder is himself a graduate of the Point, this series has the ring of authenticity as it follows the career of Clint Lane. The plots sometimes have all the excitement of anyone's daily activity, and Clint may be a model of masculine virtue, but the series will still appeal to boys with the military in mind.

REID, Alastair

    1104. Fairwater.
        Boston, Houghton Mifflin, 1957.

REID, Alastair—continued

    1105. Allth.
           Boston, Houghton Mifflin, 1958.

An excellent fantasy series for the 8 to 10 year olds. Here is the delicately truthful flavor found in true fairy tales. These stories are told with humor, suspense, and a touch of poetry.

ROBERTSON, Keith

HENRY REED SERIES

    1106. Henry Reed, Inc.
          New York, Viking, 1958.
    1107. Henry Reed's Journey.
          New York, Viking, 1963.
    1108. Henry Reed's Babysitting Service.
          New York, Viking, 1966.
    1109. Henry Reed's Big Show.
          New York, Viking, 1970.

An outstanding, outrageously funny series about inventive, adventurous Henry Reed. Excellent for boys and reluctant readers.

NEIL LAMBERT AND THE CARSON ST. DETECTIVES SERIES

    1110. The Mystery of Burnt Hill.
          New York, Viking, 1953.
    1111. Three Stuffed Owls.
          New York, Viking, 1956.
    1112. The Crow and the Castle.
          New York, Viking, 1957.
    1113. The Money Machine.
          New York, Viking, 1969.

Here is an excellent mystery series with both fun and intrigue. For boys 10 to 12 or older.

ROUNDS, Glen

WHITEY THE COWBOY SERIES

    1114. Whitey and the Blizzard.
          New York, Holiday, 1952.

ROUNDS, Glen—continued

    1115. Whitey Takes a Trip.
          New York, Holiday, 1954.
    1116. Whitey Ropes and Rides.
          New York, Holiday, 1956.
    1117. Whitey and the Wild Horse.
          New York, Holiday, 1958.
    1118. Whitey's First Roundup.
          New York, Holiday, 1960.
    1119. Whitey and the Colt Killer.
          New York, Holiday, 1962.
    1120. Whitey's New Saddle.
          New York, Holiday, 1963.

These cowboy stories are done with Mr. Rounds' usual competence. Aimed at the 8 to 10 age level, only a few of them are necessary to represent the Wild West in a collection.

RUGH, Belle

    1121. Crystal Mountain.
          Boston, Houghton Mifflin, 1955.
    1122. The Path Above the Pines.
          Boston, Houghton Mifflin, 1962.

The unusual Lebanese setting adds interest to these already intriguing mystery stories. The characterizations are well done, and the presentation of Arabs is sympathetic. Both action and humor will be found here.

SACHS, Marilyn

    VERONICA GANZ SERIES
    1123. Veronica Ganz.
          New York, Doubleday, 1968.
    1124. Peter and Veronica.
          New York, Doubleday, 1969.

    Related to series:

    1125. Marv.
          New York, Doubleday, 1970.

Ms. Sachs has a tremendous ability to write in the vernacular of the modern child. She also manages to capture his feelings and problems. These are

SACHS, Marilyn—continued

books that any girl will identify with. Veronica's problems with Peter and how they finally become friends are handled sympathetically and realistically.

AMY AND LAURA SERIES

1126. Amy Moves In.
   New York, Doubleday, 1964.
1127. Laura's Luck.
   New York, Doubleday, 1965.
1128. Amy and Laura.
   New York, Doubleday, 1966.

Another series about two sisters done with freshness and humor. Dialogue is natural, as are the situations and the characters.

SANDBURG, Helga

1129. Blueberry.
   New York, Dial, 1963.
1130. Gingerbread.
   New York, Dial, 1964.

These are horse stories with Kristen, an adolescent girl, getting her own horse. The second book finds her caring for a blind horse. The dialogue and family relationships are naturally presented, placing these two stories a little above the average horse saga.

SCHEALER, John

ZIP-ZIP SERIES

1131. Zip-Zip and His Flying Saucer.
   New York, Dutton, 1956.
1132. Zip-Zip Goes to Venus.
   New York, Dutton, 1958.
1133. Zip-Zip and the Red Planet.
   New York, Dutton, 1961.

This is an entertaining, humorous science fiction series for the 8 to 10 age group. Aficionadoes might be offended at the levity.

SELDEN, George (pseud.)
   See THOMPSON, George Selden

SHAFTNER, Dorothy

    1134. Kim Fashions a Career.
            New York, Putnam, 1968.
    1135. Kim in Style.
            New York, Putnam, 1971.

Here is another teenage career series. This one follows Kim into her career as a fashion designer. One interesting aspect of the first book is that it shows the difficulties that Kim faces in adjusting from her life at college to her life as a career girl. Generally well done and of interest to teenage readers from grades 6 to 9.

SHARP, Margery

    MISS BIANCA SERIES
    1136. The Rescuers.
            Boston, Little, 1959.
    1137. Miss Bianca.
            Boston, Little, 1962.
    1138. The Turret.
            Boston, Little, 1963.
    1139. Miss Bianca in the Salt Mines.
            Boston, Little, 1966.
    1140. Miss Bianca in the Orient.
            Boston, Little, 1970.
    1141. Miss Bianca in the Antarctic.
            Boston, Little, 1971.

This is an endearing fantasy on its way to becoming a classic. Miss Bianca, the mouse, and her friends face hair-raising adventures. There is gentle satire, too, and Garth Williams' illustrations are as exciting as ever.

SHERBURNE, Zoa

    1142. Almost April.
            New York, Morrow, 1956.
    1143. Ballerina on Skates.
            New York, Morrow, 1961.

Karen Hale is a girl with problems: she is living with her divorced father and his new wife, and Karen is tall. Her adjustment to these two situations and her attempts to find a career for herself are delineated in these two books. While the parent-child relationship may seem somewhat outdated to

SHERBURNE, Zoa—continued

today's readers, her problems are still more real than ever to these same readers. For ages 12 to 14.

SHIRREFFS, Gordon

    1144. The Cold Seas Beyond.
           Philadelphia, Westminster, 1963.
    1145. The Hostile Beaches.
           Philadelphia, Westminster, 1964.
    1146. The Enemy Seas.
           Philadelphia, Westminster, 1965.
    1147. Torpedoes Away!
           Philadelphia, Westminster, 1967.

This series follows the World War II adventures of Bob Dunbar and Gary Lunt. They find themselves aboard Navy submarines in the Aleutians and in the South Pacific as coast watchers. There are not any series set during this time that do follow wartime adventures, so this one might be a good addition for readers interested in this period of history.

SIMPSON, Dorothy

    JANIE MARSHALL SERIES

    1148. The Honest Dollar.
           Philadelphia, Lippincott, 1957.
    1149. A Lesson for Janie.
           Philadelphia, Lippincott, 1958.
    1150. A Matter of Pride.
           Philadelphia, Lippincott, 1959.
    1151. New Horizons.
           Philadelphia, Lippincott, 1961.
    1152. Visitor from the Sea.
           Philadelphia, Lippincott, 1965.

This is a good series about a girl growing up on an island off the coast of Maine. Some of her problems when she goes to school on the mainland are dealt with very effectively.

SLEIGH, Barbara

CARBONEL SERIES
1153. Carbonel, The King of the Cats.
       Indianapolis, Bobbs-Merrill, 1957.
1154. The Kingdom of Carbonel.
       Indianapolis, Bobbs-Merrill, 1960.

An excellent fantasy series about the cat, Carbonel, and his adventures. There is charming humor and magic, too, that will entrance the 9 to 12 set.

SLOBODKIN, Louis

SPACESHIP SERIES
1155. The Spaceship Under the Apple Tree.
       New York, Macmillan, 1952.
1156. The Spaceship Returns to the Apple Tree.
       New York, Macmillan, 1958.
1157. Three-Seated Spaceship.
       New York, Macmillan, 1962.
1158. Round Trip Spaceship.
       New York, Macmillan, 1968.

This is an entertaining science fiction series for those 8 to 10. Mr. Slobodkin's impressionistic illustrations greatly add to the fun.

SMITH, Dodie

1159. The Hundred and One Dalmations.
       New York, Viking, 1956.
1160. The Starlight Barking.
       New York, Viking, 1968.

Both mysteries are great fun, with an offhand, teasing style of writing that is captivating. The second book depends less on physical action than on metaphysical thoughts, but it should be popular with readers of the first book. Reluctant readers can be led to the series by the Walt Disney movie.

SMITH, Eunice

1161. The Jennifer Wish.
       Indianapolis, Bobbs-Merrill, 1949.

SMITH, Eunice—continued

    1162. The Jennifer Gift.
           Indianapolis, Bobbs-Merrill, 1950.
    1163. The Jennifer Prize.
           Indianapolis, Bobbs-Merrill, 1951.
    1164. Jennifer Is Eleven.
           Indianapolis, Bobbs-Merrill, 1952.
    1165. Jennifer Dances.
           Indianapolis, Bobbs-Merrill, 1954.
    1166. High Heels for Jennifer.
           Indianapolis, Bobbs-Merrill, 1964.

These are family stories about a young girl at the turn of the century. The happenings of her everyday life are the main subjects of the books. The reader follows her from age 8 until she becomes a teenager. This is an enjoyable series for ages 10 and up.

SMITH, Sarah

    1167. The Ink Bottle Club.
           New York, Watts, 1967.
    1168. The Ink Bottle Club Abroad.
           New York, Watts, 1969.

The parents of the children in the Ink Bottle Club tell them various stories, all unrelated. These books are held together simply by each parent's child being a member of the club. The stories are generally appealing, but not earthshaking.

SOBOL, Donald J.

    ENCYCLOPEDIA BROWN SERIES
    1169. Encyclopedia Brown, Boy Detective.
           New York, Nelson, 1963.
    1170. Encyclopedia Brown and the Case of the Secret Pitch.
           New York, Nelson, 1965.
    1171. Encyclopedia Brown Finds the Clues.
           New York, Nelson, 1966.
    1172. Encyclopedia Brown Gets His Man.
           New York, Nelson, 1967.
    1173. Encyclopedia Brown Solves Them All.
           New York, Nelson, 1968.

SOBOL, Donald J.—continued

    1174. Encyclopedia Brown Keeps the Peace.
           New York, Nelson, 1969.
    1175. Encyclopedia Brown Saves the Day.
           New York, Nelson, 1970.
    1176. Encyclopedia Brown Tracks Them Down.
           New York, Nelson, 1971.

This is a clever and amusing mystery series for younger readers. Each book contains a series of cases, so even reluctant readers and those with a short attention span should be able to handle them.

SOMMERFELT, Aimee

    LALU SERIES
    1177. The Road to Agra.
           New York, Criterion, 1961.
    1178. The White Bungalow.
           New York, Criterion, 1964.

Moving, tense stories about the determined boy Lalu and the decisions he makes. The first book tells about his taking his blind sister to Agra to have her sight restored. The second deals with his dilemma of whether to accept a scholarship to go away to school or stay in his village and help his family. For the mature reader.

SPEARING, Judith

    1179. Ghosts Who Went to School.
           New York, Atheneum, 1966.
    1180. The Museum House Ghosts.
           New York, Atheneum, 1969.

In this series, the ghosts are the main characters and the humor of the situation is fully developed. Ghosts Mortimer and Wilbur have difficulty behaving like human beings, since they are not, and have no idea how to cope with modern fashions, cliches, and behavior. A better-than-average bet for readers 8 to 12.

SPENCE, Eleanor

    1181. The Switherby Pilgrims.
           New York, Roy, 1967.

SPENCE, Elizabeth—continued

    1182. Jamberoo Road.
          New York, Roy, 1969.

A group of ten orphans moves from England to Australia during the 1800s. These books follow their adventures in the outback. The second book continues the story of each child into adulthood. The background atmosphere is quite good, and the depiction of pioneer life in Australia outstanding. The Australian dialect is not used excessively, so there should be no problem for readers from seventh grade on up.

SPRAGUE, Gretchen

    1183. A Question of Harmony.
          New York, Dodd, 1965.
    1184. White in the Moon.
          New York, Dodd, 1968.

Two girls, one white, one black, are brought together by their love of music. In their relationship, they encounter racial prejudice from outsiders. A thought-provoking series for the teenage reader.

SPYKMAN, E. C.

    CARES FAMILY SERIES

    1185. A Lemon and a Star.
          New York, Harcourt, 1955.
    1186. The Wild Angel.
          New York, Harcourt, 1957.
    1187. Terrible, Horrible Edie.
          New York, Harcourt, 1960.
    1188. Edie on the Warpath.
          New York, Harcourt, 1966.

Well-handled, lively, and humorous period stories of family life. Sibling relationships are realistically depicted. The second book is somewhat slow-moving, but still good. The last two are especially hilarious.

STAHL, Ben

    BLACKBEARD SERIES

    1189. Blackbeard's Ghost.
          Boston, Houghton Mifflin, 1965.

STAHL, Ben—continued

    1190. The Secret of Red Skull.
            Boston, Houghton Mifflin, 1971.

These wild fantasies follow the adventures of Blackbeard's ghost, who has come to life again. There is an odd mixture of witchcraft and spies in the second book that calls for quite a suspension of disbelief on the part of the reader.

STOLZ, Mary

    BARKHAM ST. SERIES
    1191. A Dog on Barkham St.
            New York, Harper, 1960.
    1192. The Bully of Barkham St.
            New York, Harper, 1963.

This is a beautifully conceived series. The first book is about the boys on Barkham St., and various adventures and problems they have, including those with a bully. The second book takes the same situation from the side of the bully. An interesting idea done with humor and understanding.

    MORGAN CONNOR SERIES
    1193. Ready or Not.
            New York, Harper, 1953.
    1194. The Day and the Way We Met.
            New York, Harper, 1956.

Basically romances, these books are written on a simple enough level to interest girls 10 to 12. The second book is inferior to the first because too many characters are introduced without focusing sharply enough on any one.

    1195. Belling the Tiger.
            New York, Harper, 1961.
    1196. The Great Rebellion.
            New York, Harper, 1961.
    1197. Siri the Conquistador.
            New York, Harper, 1963.

An excellent series about two mice, Asa and Rambo, and their various exploits. Told with good humor, these tales for the 8 to 10 set also show a wry reflection on human foibles.

STORR, Catherine

    1198. Lucy.
        New York, Prentice, 1968.
    1199. Lucy Runs Away.
        New York, Prentice, 1969.

Young Lucy will appeal to many girls today who would rather picture themselves in the midst of hair-raising adventures than home playing with dolls. She fancies herself a dashing outlaw and proceeds to act accordingly, getting herself into numerous difficulties. Good for reading aloud, told with humor and understanding. For girls 8 to 12.

STYLES, Showell

    1200. Midshipman Quinn.
        New York, Vanguard, 1958.
    1201. Quinn of the "Fury."
        New York, Vanguard, 1961.
    1202. Midshipman Quinn and Denise the Spy.
        New York, Vanguard, 1963.
    1203. Quinn at Trafalgar.
        New York, Vanguard, 1968.

An above-average history-adventure series, this one concerns Septimus Quinn, a member of Admiral Nelson's fleet. Wittier than most, with some attention paid to battle strategy, this should be a favorite for boys 11 to 14.

SUMNER, Cid Ricketts

    1204. Tammy Out of Time.
        Indianapolis, Bobbs-Merrill, 1948.
    1205. Tammy Tell Me True.
        Indianapolis, Bobbs-Merrill, 1959.

This series was made into the numerous "Tammy" films. They follow the adventures of a girl from a shantyboat who goes to college. Her backwoods mannerisms bring on both snobbery and affection in those she meets. For readers 14 and up.

SWIFT, Helen

    1206. First Semester.
        New York, Longmans, 1960.

SWIFT, Helen—continued

    1207. Second Semester.
          New York, Longmans, 1961.

This series follows Betsy and Jan into college, covering their problems in adapting to college life during their first year. They have the usual problems and romances to be found in other novels of this ilk. Not particularly outstanding.

SYMONS, Geraldine

    1208. The Workhouse Child.
          New York, Macmillan, 1969.
    1209. Miss Rivers and Miss Bridges.
          New York, Macmillan, 1971.

Sheltered Pansy and brusque Atalanta join forces to rescue a workhouse child and Pansy winds up in the workhouse herself. They later move on to become unofficial members of the Suffragette movement in England. Told with a winning humor, the girls are both human and appealing. A better-than-average series for readers 9 to 12.

TAYLOR, Don

    1210. Old Sam, Thoroughbred Trotter.
          Chicago, Follett, 1955.
    1211. Old Sam and the Horse Thieves.
          Chicago, Follett, 1967.

In a typical plot, two boys turn their work horse into a champion trotting horse. This same horse goes on to even bigger adventures. Certainly not an unusual series, this one is mediocre. Not really necessary.

TAYLOR, Sydney

    ALL-OF-A-KIND FAMILY SERIES
    1212. All-of-a-Kind Family.
          Chicago, Follett, 1951.
    1213. More All-of-a-Kind Family.
          Chicago, Follett, 1954.
    1214. All-of-a-Kind Family Uptown.
          Chicago, Follett, 1958.

TAYLOR, Sydney—continued

    1215. All-of-a-Kind Family Downtown.
          Chicago, Follett, 1972.

These are warm stories about a Jewish family with five girls, set in New York City at the turn of the century. Characterizations are excellent, family relationships are treated realistically, and there is much humor. Mary Stevens' illustrations will enchant girl readers.

THOMPSON, George Selden (pseud., George Selden)

    1216. The Cricket in Times Square.
          New York, Farrar, 1960.
    1217. Tucker's Countryside.
          New York, Farrar, 1969.

This is a good series about a cricket in New York and his friends. There is warmth and humor, and in the second book, a strong plea for conservation.

THOMPSON, Mary Wolfe

    AIKEN FAMILY SERIES
    1218. Two in the Wilderness.
          New York, McKay, 1967.
    1219. Wilderness Winter.
          New York, McKay, 1968.
    1220. Wilderness Wedding.
          New York, McKay, 1970.

Set in colonial Vermont, this series grows up with the readers, following Mary from girlhood to her marriage. The second volume lacks the spontaneity and interest of the first.

THOMSON, Peter

    1221. Sierra Ranger.
          New York, Dodd, 1954.
    1222. Ski Ranger.
          New York, Dodd, 1957.

Doug Moran is an apprentice in the National Park Service. On his various assignments, he falls into many adventures. The background material on forestry is good, and the series benefits from this unusual background. An unusual choice for career-oriented readers.

TITUS, Eve

> BASIL SERIES
> 1223. Basil of Baker St.
> > New York, McGraw, 1958.
> 1224. Basil and the Lost Colony.
> > New York, McGraw, 1964.
> 1225. Basil and the Pygmy Cats.
> > New York, McGraw, 1971.

Here is an amusing series about a mouse who lives in Sherlock Holmes's flat and models himself after Holmes. The drawings by Paul Galdone add zest to the lively plots.

TODD, Ruthven

> SPACE CAT SERIES
> 1226. Space Cat.
> > New York, Scribner, 1952.
> 1227. Space Cat Visits Venus.
> > New York, Scribner, 1955.
> 1228. Space Cat Meets Mars.
> > New York, Scribner, 1957.
> 1229. Space Cat and the Kittens.
> > New York, Scribner, 1958.

This is an amusing series of pseudo-science fiction, but in the face of recent developments in space exploration, it might seem hopelessly outdated to young readers today.

TOMERLIN, John

> 1230. The Magnificent Jalopy.
> > New York, Dutton, 1967.
> 1231. The Nothing Special.
> > New York, Dutton, 1969.

For a summer project, three boys buy a 1936 Packard, renovate it, and enter it in an old car rally. The next book finds them working on another car. The writing is sparkling, the characters individuals, and the plots just a little different from the usual boy-meets-car story. For ages 11 up.

TREECE, Henry

        HARALD SIGURDSON SERIES

    1232. Viking's Dawn.
            New York, Criterion, 1956.
    1233. The Road to Miklagard.
            New York, Criterion, 1957.
    1234. Viking's Sunset.
            New York, Criterion, 1961.

An outstanding trilogy about Viking Harald Sigurdson's various trips (Russia and America among them). They have the true vigor and drama of a saga. Exciting for 10 year olds on up.

        HARDRADA TRILOGY SERIES

    1235. Man with a Sword.
            New York, Pantheon, 1964.
    1236. The Last Viking.
            New York, Pantheon, 1966.
    1237. Swords from the North.
            New York, Pantheon, 1967.

More tales by the master storyteller about the Vikings. Mr. Treece portrays the heroism, ironic humor, and fierce loyalty of these men better than any other writer. Highly recommended.

TUDOR, Tasha

    1238. Becky's Birthday.
            New York, Viking, 1960.
    1239. Becky's Christmas.
            New York, Viking, 1961.

Ms. Tudor is best known for her pastel illustrations. These books take full advantage of her talent in presenting the quiet family story of Becky. The simplicity of life about 50 years ago is admirably reflected in her drawings. This will be a good series, both to read aloud and for beginning readers, grades 2 to 4.

TURNER, Philip

    1240. Colonel Shepperton's Clock.
            Cleveland, World, 1966.

TURNER, Philip—continued

    1241. The Grange at High Force.
           Cleveland, World, 1967.
    1242. Steam on the Line.
           Cleveland, World, 1968.

The first book begins the story with the grandfather of David, the chief character in the last two books. They're combination mystery-adventures with more substance than is common to members of that genre. There is humor, wit, strong characterizations, as well as unusual background (an ecclesiastical setting for a mystery!). The third member of this series won the Carnegie Medal. For ages 10 to 14.

UNNERSTAD, Edith

    LARSSON FAMILY SERIES

    1243. The Saucepan Journey.
        Translated by James Harker
           New York, Macmillan, 1951.
    1244. Pysen.
        Translated by James Harker
           New York, Macmillan, 1955.
    1245. Little O.
        Translated by Inger Boye
           New York, Macmillan, 1957.
    1246. The Peep-Larssons Go Sailing.
        Translated by Lilian Seaton
           New York, Macmillan, 1962.

Warm family relationships are established in this Swedish series. The books show humor, adventure, and a warm knowledge of human foibles.

VAN CLIEF, Sylvia
    See HEIDE, Florence

VAN STOCKUM, Hilda

    MITCHELL FAMILY SERIES

    1247. The Mitchells.
           New York, Viking, 1945.

VAN STOCKUM, Hilda—continued

    1248. Canadian Summer.
          New York, Viking, 1948.
    1249. Friendly Gables.
          New York, Viking, 1960.

An excellent series about family life in Canada. An entertaining, yet realistic picture. Especially good for girls 9 to 12.

VARNEY, Joyce

    TWM TYBACH AND JOEY SERIES

    1250. The Magic Maker.
          Indianapolis, Bobbs-Merrill, 1967.
    1251. The Half-Time Gypsy.
          Indianapolis, Bobbs-Merrill, 1968.

These fantasies combine Welsh charm and larger-than-life characters to add to the appeal for kids 9 to 12. The second book should appeal to boys; Joey wants gypsy freedom but, finding that it has drawbacks, settles for being a half-time gypsy.

VERNEY, John

    CALLENDER FAMILY SERIES

    1252. Friday's Tunnel.
          New York, Holt, 1959.
    1253. February's Road.
          New York, Holt, 1961.
    1254. Ismo.
          New York, Holt, 1964.
    1255. Seven Sunflower Seeds.
          New York, Holt, 1968.

Another good series about family life. These again are for more mature readers. The humor has adult sarcasm. No goody-goody family, this.

VIPONT, Elfrida

    1256. The Lark in the Morn.
          New York, Holt, 1970.

VIPONT, Elfrida—continued

    1257. The Lark on the Wing.
            New York, Holt, 1970.
    1258. The Pavilion.
            New York, Holt, 1970.

Another family series—the Haverards and Kitsons—but with a variation. The families are Quakers, and each story has a musical background. Competent and appealing, especially for girls 11 to 14.

WAHL, Jan

    PLEASANT FIELDMOUSE SERIES

    1259. Pleasant Fieldmouse.
            New York, Harper, 1964.
    1260. The Six Voyages of Pleasant Fieldmouse.
            New York, Delacorte, 1971.

The first volume of this series was most enjoyable, with freshness and spontaneity. Unfortunately, the second is a tremendous disappointment. The plot is tedious, the humor and the dialogue lack vividness. Nothing to recommend it.

WALDEN, Amelia

    MIRANDA WELCH SERIES

    1261. When Love Speaks.
            New York, Whittlesey, 1961.
    1262. So Near the Heart.
            New York, Whittlesey, 1962.
    1263. My World's the Stage.
            New York, Whittlesey, 1964.

These are agreeable romances for mature youngsters or early teens. Especially interesting for girls is the last one, which has a theatrical setting.

    CAROL TURNER SERIES

    1264. Where Is My Heart.
            Philadelphia, Westminster, 1960.
    1265. How Bright the Dawn.
            Philadelphia, Westminster, 1962.

More romances, this time rather trite.

WALDEN, Amelia—continued

    1266. The Case of the Diamond Eye.
           Philadelphia, Westminster, 1969.
    1267. What Happened to Candy Carmichael?
           Philadelphia, Westminster, 1970.
    1268. Valerie Valentine Is Missing.
           Philadelphia, Westminster, 1971.

Here is another mystery series with a girl detective, Lisa Clark. Set in foreign lands, they are smoothly written, fast-paced, lightweight material for readers 10 to 14.

WALTER, Mildred

    1269. Lillie of Watts: A Birthday Discovery.
           New York, Ritchie, 1969.
    1270. Lillie of Watts Takes a Giant Step.
           New York, Doubleday, 1971.

A young Negro girl from the Watts section of Los Angeles tries to adjust to her situation. This series gives a realistic portrait of the life style and attitudes of young blacks in a ghetto. For grades 5 on up.

WALTERS, Hugh, pseud. (Hughes, Walter Llewellyn)

    1271. Blast-Off at 0300.
           New York, Criterion, 1958.
    1272. Menace From the Moon.
           New York, Criterion, 1959.
    1273. First on the Moon.
           New York, Criterion, 1960.
    1274. Outpost on the Moon.
           New York, Criterion, 1962.
    1275. Expedition Venus.
           New York, Criterion, 1963.
    1276. Terror by Satellite.
           New York, Criterion, 1964.
    1277. Mission to Mercury.
           New York, Criterion, 1965.
    1278. Journey to Jupiter.
           New York, Criterion, 1966.

WALTERS, Hugh—continued

    1279. Spaceship to Saturn.
             New York, Criterion, 1967.
    1280. The Mohole Menace.
             New York, Criterion, 1968.
    1281. Neptune One Is Missing.
             New York, Washburn, 1969.

This is a science fiction series featuring Chris Godfrey. The plots are generally fast-moving, situations relatively plausible. However, there is some repetition in plot, so the whole series is not necessary to a collection.

WARNER, Gertrude Chandler

    BOXCAR CHILDREN SERIES OR ALDEN FAMILY SERIES

    1282. The Boxcar Children.
             Chicago, Scott, 1950.
    1283. Surprise Island.
             Chicago, Scott, 1949.
    1284. The Yellow House Mystery.
             Chicago, Scott, 1953.
    1285. Mystery Ranch.
             Chicago, Scott, 1958.
    1286. Mike's Mystery.
             Chicago, Scott, 1960.
    1287. Blue Bay Mystery.
             Chicago, Scott, 1961.
    1288. The Woodshed Mystery.
             Chicago, Scott, 1962.
    1289. The Lighthouse Mystery.
             Chicago, Scott, 1963.
    1290. Mountain Top Mystery.
             Chicago, Scott, 1964.
    1291. Schoolhouse Mystery.
             Chicago, Scott, 1965.
    1292. Caboose Mystery.
             Chicago, Whitman, 1966.
    1293. Houseboat Mystery.
             Chicago, Whitman, 1967.
    1294. Snowbound Mystery.
             Chicago, Whitman, 1968.
    1295. Tree House Mystery.
             Chicago, Whitman, 1969.

WARNER, Gertrude Chandler—continued

    1296. Bicycle Mystery.
            Chicago, Whitman, 1971.
    1297. Mystery in the Sand.
            Chicago, Whitman, 1971.

The first two books of the series are outstanding, especially *The Boxcar Children*, about an orphaned family who takes to a boxcar in an attempt to stay together and not be put in an orphanage. The series then becomes simply a series of mystery stories, all of which are popular with the children, even though they do not show the same originality and high quality of writing as the first. Good for reluctant readers.

WARNLOF, Anna Lisa

    1298. The Boy Upstairs.
            Translated by Annabelle MacMillan
            New York, Harcourt, 1961.
    1299. Frederika's Children.
            Translated by Annabelle MacMillan
            New York, Harcourt, 1962.

The strong point of this series lies in the very realistic portrayal of its characters. Frederika and Martin are neighbors, and the books alternate between her point of view and his, giving the reader both sides of the picture. She can be unpleasant, self-centered, jealous, but also appealing. For more mature readers from 8 to 12.

WEALES, Gerald

    1300. Miss Grimsbee Is a Witch.
            Philadelphia, Lippincott, 1957.
    1301. Miss Grimsbee Takes a Vacation.
            Philadelphia, Lippincott, 1965.

Miss Grimsbee has the appealing blend of gentleness and self-centeredness that makes for the most entertaining type of fantasy character. These books combine fantasy with everyday life, balancing these two elements nicely. Told with humor, these are favorites with ages 8 to 12.

WEBER, Lenora Mattingly

STACY BELFORD SERIES

1302. Don't Call Me Katie Rose.
New York, Crowell, 1964.
1303. The Winds of March.
New York, Crowell, 1965.
1304. A New and Different Summer.
New York, Crowell, 1966.
1305. I Met a Boy I Used to Know.
New York, Crowell, 1967.
1306. Angel in Heavy Shoes.
New York, Crowell, 1968.
1307. How Long Is Always?
New York, Crowell, 1970.
1308. Hello, My Love, Goodbye.
New York, Crowell, 1971.
1309. Sometimes a Stranger.
New York, Crowell, 1972.

Another family romance series. The first few are good for mature younger readers and help bridge the gap to young adult books. All are written on a simple level.

BEANY MALONE SERIES

1310. Meet the Malones.
New York, Crowell, 1943.
1311. Beany Malone.
New York, Crowell, 1948.
1312. Leave It to Beany.
New York, Crowell, 1950.
1313. Beany and the Beckoning Road.
New York, Crowell, 1952.
1314. Beany Has a Secret Life.
New York, Crowell, 1955.
1315. Make a Wish for Me.
New York, Crowell, 1956.
1316. Happy Birthday, Dear Beany.
New York, Crowell, 1957.
1317. The More the Merrier.
New York, Crowell, 1958.
1318. A Bright Star Falls.
New York, Crowell, 1959.

WEBER, Lenora Mattingly—continued

  1319. Welcome, Stranger.
     New York, Crowell, 1960.
  1320. Pick a New Dream.
     New York, Crowell, 1961.
  1321. Tarry Awhile.
     New York, Crowell, 1962.
  1322. Something Borrowed, Something Blue.
     New York, Crowell, 1963.
  1323. Come Back, Wherever You Are.
     New York, Crowell, 1969.

Much the same as the Stacy Belford series. Despite its age, this one still retains its popularity. Again, only the first few have a subject matter of interest to the 10 to 12 girls. The rest are for the early teens.

WELCH, Ronald, pseud. (Felton, Ronald Oliver)

  CAREY FAMILY SERIES

  1324. Mohawk Valley.
     New York, Criterion, 1958.
  1325. Escape from France.
     New York, Criterion, 1961.
  1326. For the King.
     New York, Criterion, 1962.
  1327. Nicholas Carey.
     New York, Criterion, 1963.
  1328. The Hawk.
     New York, Criterion, 1969.

  Related to the series:

  1329. Bowman of Crecy.
     New York, Criterion, 1966.

A family series with a difference—the novels are historical, covering different periods and places, and the main characters are the men of the Carey family. Swashbuckling adventures, well documented. The related book is about a bowman in John Carey's command.

WELLMAN, Manly Wade

    1330. Rifles at Ramsour's Mill.
          New York, Washburn, 1961.
    1331. The Battle for King's Mountain.
          New York, Washburn, 1962.
    1332. Clash on Catawba.
          New York, Washburn, 1962.
    1333. The South Fork Rangers.
          New York, Washburn, 1963.

Set during the Revolutionary War, these are the exciting adventures of Zack Harper. Very good fare, with better-than-average historical accuracy.

    1334. Ghost Battalion.
          New York, Washburn, 1958.
    1335. Ride, Rebels.
          New York, Washburn, 1959.
    1336. Appomattox Road.
          New York, Washburn, 1960.

More historical fiction by this author, this series follows Clay Buckner of the Iron Scouts. He is a Civil War soldier on the Confederate side. Good adventure with plenty of action for boys in grades 7 to 9.

    1337. The Mystery at Bear Paw Gap.
          New York, Washburn, 1966.
    1338. Battle at Bear Paw Gap.
          New York, Washburn, 1966.
    1339. The Specter of Bear Paw Gap.
          New York, Washburn, 1966.

Yet another well-done historical series, this one is set in post-Revolutionary America. For ages 12 and up.

WELLS, Bob

    FIVE YARD FULLER SERIES
    1340. Five Yard Fuller. (Putnam Sports Shelf)
          New York, Putnam, 1964.
    1341. Five Yard Fuller of the New York Gnats. (Putnam Sports Shelf)
          New York, Putnam, 1967.

WELLS, Bob—continued

    1342. Five Yard Fuller and the Unlikely Knights. (Putnam Sports Shelf)
        New York, Putnam, 1967.
    1343. Five Yard Fuller's Mighty Model T. (Putnam Sports Shelf)
        New York, Putnam, 1970.

Humorous sports stories that will appeal to boys 9 to 12. Details about football are very true-to-life as well.

WEST, Emmy
    See GOVAN, Christine

WEST, Nick

    ALFRED HITCHCOCK AND THE THREE INVESTIGATORS SERIES
    (See also entries under William Arden, M. V. Carey, and Robert Arthur)

    1344. Alfred Hitchcock and the Three Investigators in the Mystery of the Coughing Dragon. No. 14.
        New York, Random House, 1970.
    1345. Alfred Hitchcock and the Three Investigators in the Mystery of the Nervous Lion. No. 15.
        New York, Random House, 1971.

The same mystery formula as the other members of the series.

WESTREICH, Budd

    DEREK MORGAN

    1346. The Day It Rained Sidneys.
        New York, McKay, 1965.
    1347. Please Stand Clear of the Apache Arrows.
        New York, McKay, 1969.

Amusing adventure-mysteries, this series has wit and flavor that will appeal to boys, and surprise endings to boot.

WIBBERLY, Leonard (pseud. Patrick O'Connor)

WARNER FAMILY SERIES
1348. Seawind from Hawaii.
New York, Washburn, 1965.
1349. Beyond Hawaii.
New York, Washburn, 1969.

These books cover the adventures of a family which sails in and around Hawaii. The descriptions of the islands and the joys of sailing are among the high points. The sailing terminology might become confusing, however. A glossary would have helped. Nonetheless, good adventure fare.

1350. Encounter Near Venus.
New York, Farrar, 1967.
1351. Journey to Untor.
New York, Farrar, 1970.

This series combines fantasy and science fiction as Uncle Bill and his four nieces and nephews journey to other planets. Mr. Wibberly includes philosophical, religious, and ethical questions along with the adventure.
A very good series for science fiction buffs, or anyone else, for that matter.

TREEGATE FAMILY SERIES
1352. John Treegate's Musket.
New York, Farrar, 1959.
1353. Peter Treegate's War.
New York, Farrar, 1960.
1354. Sea Captain from Salem.
New York, Farrar, 1961.
1355. Treegate's Raiders.
New York, Farrar, 1962.
1356. Leopard's Prey.
New York, Farrar, 1971.

This is an excellent series about the adventures of various members of the Treegate family during the Revolutionary War. Strong vitality, exciting action, well-drawn characters, all make this an excellent bet for boys 10 to 12 or older.

BLACK TIGER SERIES
1357. Black Tiger.
New York, Farrar, 1956.
1358. Mexican Road Race.
New York, Farrar, 1956.

WIBBERLY, Leonard—continued

    1359. Black Tiger at Le Mans.
           New York, Farrar, 1958.
    1360. Black Tiger at Bonneville.
           New York, Farrar, 1960.
    1361. Black Tiger at Indianapolis.
           New York, Farrar, 1962.

A good lively series about car racing for boys. Engaging characters and humorous dialogue add to the appeal.

WILDER, Laura Ingalls

    LITTLE HOUSE SERIES
    1362. Little House in the Big Woods.
           New York, Harper, 1932.
    1363. Little House on the Prairie.
           New York, Harper, 1935.
    1364. Farmer Boy.
           New York, Harper, 1933.
    1365. On the Banks of Plum Creek.
           New York, Harper, 1937.
    1366. By the Shores of Silver Lake.
           New York, Harper, 1939.
    1367. The Long Winter.
           New York, Harper, 1940.
    1368. Little Town on the Prairie.
           New York, Harper, 1941.
    1369. These Happy Golden Years.
           Yew York, Harper, 1943.
    1370. The First Four Years.
           New York, Harper, 1971.

This autobiographical series about a young girl growing up in pioneer America is a modern classic. All to be recommended except the new volume, which is really an unfinished manuscript of Ms. Wilder's which her daughter unwisely allowed to be published. Naturally, the style is rough, and it most probably is not the polished product Ms. Wilder would have wanted read. The subject matter, dealing with famine, drought, and the loss of a child, is much more mature than the book format would suggest. Much more for teenage readers, despite the large print and Garth Williams' illustrations.

WILLARD, Barbara

    1371. The Family Tower.
          New York, Harcourt, 1968.
    1372. The Toppling Towers.
          New York, Harcourt, 1969.

A good series for older girls, this wavers sometimes perilously close to soap opera, but always has perceptive insights, strong characterizations, and good dialogue.

    BARBARA SERIES

    1373. A Dog and a Half.
          New York, Nelson, 1964.
    1374. Surprise Island.
          New York, Nelson, 1969.

Two girls have various adventures with their out-sized St. Bernard. Good fun and easy reading for ages 8 to 12.

WILLIAMS, Jay, and Raymond Abrashkin

    DANNY DUNN SERIES

    1375. Danny Dunn and the Anti-Gravity Paint.
          New York, McGraw, 1956.
    1376. Danny Dunn on a Desert Island.
          New York, McGraw, 1957.
    1377. Danny Dunn and the Homework Machine.
          New York, McGraw, 1958.
    1378. Danny Dunn and the Weather Machine.
          New York, McGraw, 1959.
    1379. Danny Dunn on the Ocean Floor.
          New York, McGraw, 1960.
    1380. Danny Dunn and the Fossil Cave.
          New York, McGraw, 1961.
    1381. Danny Dunn and the Heat Ray.
          New York, McGraw, 1962.
    1382. Danny Dunn, Time Traveler.
          New York, McGraw, 1963.
    1383. Danny Dunn and the Automatic House.
          New York, McGraw, 1965.
    1384. Danny Dunn and the Voice from Space.
          New York, McGraw, 1967.

WILLIAMS, Jay, and Raymond Abrashkin—continued

    1385. Danny Dunn and the Smallifying Machine.
          New York, McGraw, 1969.
    1386. Danny Dunn and the Swamp Monster.
          New York, McGraw, 1971.

This is a highly enjoyable series about a very inventive boy. Plots somehow manage to remain fresh and lively, with a nice, humorous touch. Especially good for boys and reluctant readers.

WILLIAMS, Ursula Moray

    1387. The Toymaker's Daughter.
          New York, Nelson, 1969.
    1388. The Three Toymakers.
          New York, Nelson, 1970.
    1389. Malkin's Mountain.
          New York, Nelson, 1972.

These stories concern a live doll, daughter of a wicked toymaker. She has a mischievous streak that does not always bode well. Characterizations are excellent and the plots have more than one level of meaning, but the second story may be too complex and contrived for the 8 to 11 age level it is aimed at.

WILSON, Ellen
    See AGLE, Nan

WILSON, Hazel

    1390. Herbert.
          New York, Knopf, 1950.
    1391. Herbert Again.
          New York, Knopf, 1951.
    1392. More Fun with Herbert.
          New York, Knopf, 1954.
    1393. Herbert's Homework.
          New York, Knopf, 1960.
    1394. Herbert's Space Trip.
          New York, Knopf, 1965.
    1395. Herbert's Stilts.
          New York, Knopf, 1972.

WILSON, Hazel—continued

Young Herbert is a rambunctious young man who manages to get himself into all kinds of far-fetched adventures, including stilts that come alive, space travel, and having an electronic brain do his homework. These will be fun for boys who enjoy zany humor. For ages 8 to 12.

WINTERFELD, Henry

>1396. Detectives in Togas.
>>Translated by Richard and Clara Winston
>>>New York, Harcourt, 1956.
>
>1397. Mystery of the Roman Ransom.
>>Translated by Edith McCormick
>>>New York, Harcourt, 1971.

An excellent series of mysteries done with wry, rollicking humor. Literate fun set in Roman times.

WOOLLEY, Catherine

>LEONARD FAMILY SERIES
>
>1398. A Room for Cathy.
>>New York, Morrow, 1956.
>1399. Miss Cathy Leonard.
>>New York, Morrow, 1958.
>1400. Cathy Leonard Calling.
>>New York, Morrow, 1960.
>1401. Cathy's Little Sister.
>>New York, Morrow, 1964.
>1402. Chris in Trouble.
>>New York, Morrow, 1968.
>1403. Cathy and the Beautiful People.
>>New York, Morrow, 1971.
>1404. Cathy Uncovers a Secret.
>>New York, Morrow, 1972.

A very well-done family series about the misadventures of two sisters. Natural situations and dialogue. For girls 8 to 10.

>LIBBY SERIES
>
>1405. Look Alive, Libby!
>>New York, Morrow, 1962.

WOOLLEY, Catherine—continued

    1406. Libby Looks for a Spy.
        New York, Morrow, 1965.
    1407. Libby's Uninvited Guest.
        New York, Morrow, 1970.

Another pleasant series by Ms. Woolley, this time set in New England.

    GINNIE SERIES
    1408. Ginnie and Geneva.
        New York, Morrow, 1948.
    1409. Ginnie Joins In.
        New York, Morrow, 1951.
    1410. Ginnie and the New Girl.
        New York, Morrow, 1954.
    1411. Ginnie and the Mystery House.
        New York, Morrow, 1957.
    1412. Ginnie and the Mystery Doll.
        New York, Morrow, 1960.
    1413. Ginnie and Her Juniors.
        New York, Morrow, 1963.
    1414. Ginnie and the Cooking Contest.
        New York, Morrow, 1966.
    1415. Ginnie and the Wedding Bells.
        New York, Morrow, 1967.
    1416. Ginnie and the Mystery Cat.
        New York, Morrow, 1969.

This is another charming series for younger girls. Most of the stories are gay and delightful, but *Ginnie and Her Juniors* suffers from a slight, dull plot. Not as inventive as the others.

    DAVID SERIES
    1417. David's Railroad.
        New York, Morrow, 1949.
    1418. Holiday on Wheels.
        New York, Morrow, 1953.
    1419. David's Hundred Dollars.
        New York, Morrow, 1952.
    1420. David's Campaign Buttons.
        New York, Morrow, 1959.

This is an easy-to-read series that follows young David through assorted adventures. The books have a factual base—i.e., the workings of government

WOOLLEY, Catherine—continued

in the campaign story, railroads, etc.—that is especially useful in painlessly acquainting children with the world around them. Unfortunately, the series is out of print.

WORK, Rhoda O.

    1421. Mr. Dawson Had a Farm.
           Indianapolis, Bobbs-Merrill, 1951.
    1422. Mr. Dawson Had an Elephant.
           Indianapolis, Bobbs-Merrill, 1959.
    1423. Mr. Dawson Had a Lamb.
           Indianapolis, Bobbs-Merrill, 1963.

These are humorous, easy-to-read misadventures of the unlucky Mr. Dawson. The difficulties he gets himself into have a slapstick overtone that may not appeal to every reader. Still, those in grades 3 to 5 might enjoy this series.

YORK, Andrew
    See NICOLE, Christopher, pseud.

YORK, Carol Beach

    BUTTERFIELD SQUARE SERIES
    1424. Miss Know-It-All.
           New York, Watts, 1966.
    1425. The Christmas Dolls.
           New York, Watts, 1967.
    1426. The Good Day Mice.
           New York, Watts, 1968.
    1427. Good Charlotte.
           New York, Watts, 1969.
    1428. The Ten O'Clock Club.
           New York, Watts, 1970.

These are the adventures of various orphan girls who live in a home on Butterfield Square. The stories are humorous, as are the characters. The books also benefit from the charming illustrations.

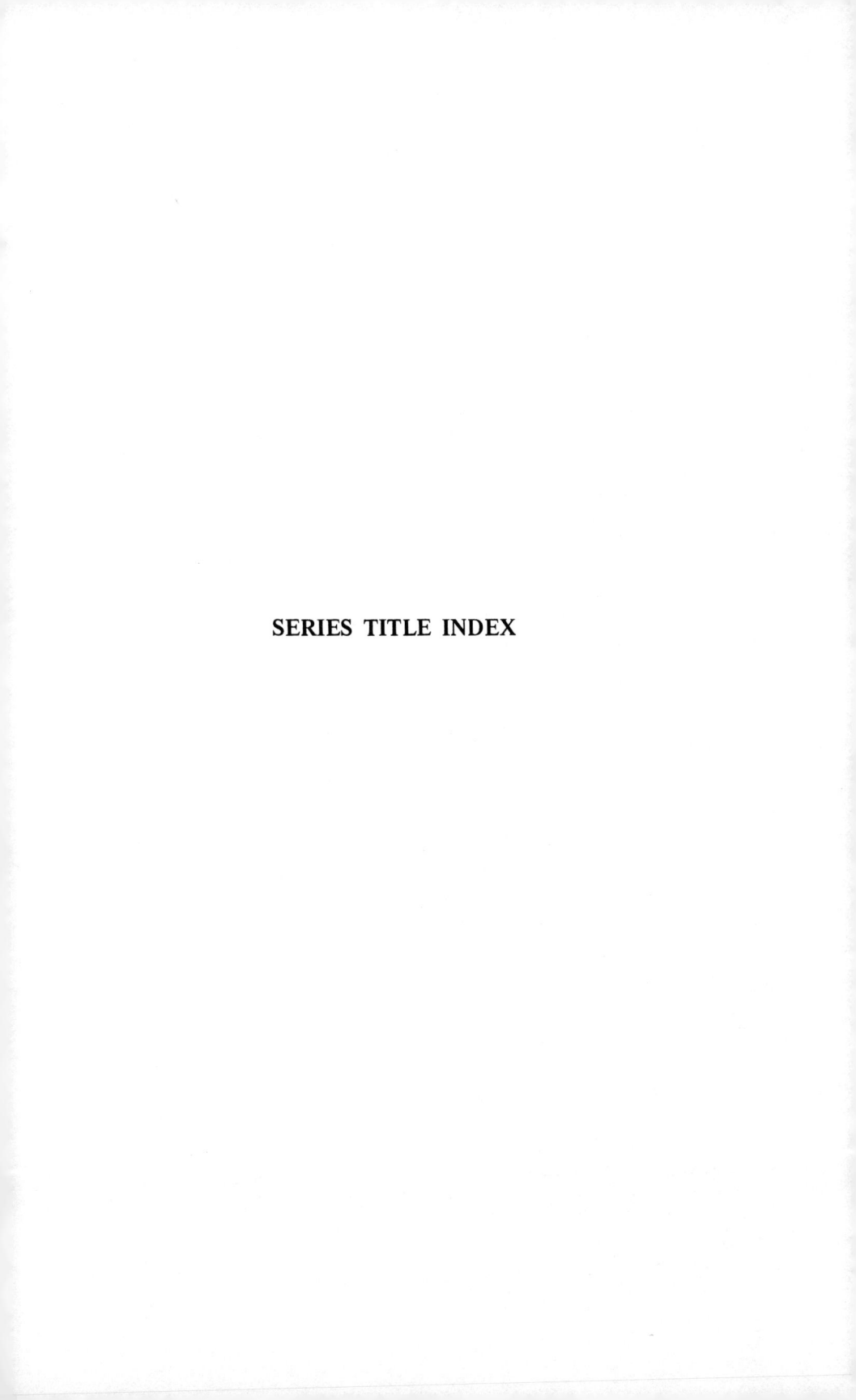

SERIES TITLE INDEX

SERIES TITLE INDEX

Agaton Sax Series, 549-551
Aiken Family Series, 1218-1220
Alden Family Series, 1282-1297
Alfred Hitchcock Series, 49-52, 55-64, 244-245, 1344-1345
All-of-a-Kind Family Series, 1212-1215
Alvin Fernald Series, 660-663
Amy and Laura Series, 1126-1128
Anna Lavinia Series, 215-216
Annegret Series, 113-115
Aunt Vinnie Series, 45-46
Austin Family Series, 799-802
Ayyar Series, 987-988
Azor Series, 361-364

Badge Lorenny Series, 273-275
Barbara Series, 1373-1374
Barker Family Series, 1065-1067
Barkham St. Series, 1191-1192
Basil Series, 1223-1225
Beany Malone Series, 1310-1323
Beebe Family Series, 651-653
Betsy and Eddie Series, 624-646
Bill Bergson Series, 820-822
Birdy Jones Series, 666-667
Black Stallion Series, 504-517
Black Tiger Series, 1357-1361
Blackbeard Series, 1189-1190
Bonnie Series, 259-262
Borrowers Series, 996-1000
Boxcar Children Series, 1282-1297
Brad Thomas Series, 924-929
Bread-and-Butter Series, 316-317
Brogeen Series, 839-841
Bronc Burnett Series, 863-886
Brumby Series, 1031-1032
Bud Baker Series, 695-701
Butterfield Square Series, 1424-1428

Callender Family Series, 1252-1255
Cameron Family Series, 437-441
Cammie Series, 895-897
Campbell Family Series, 765-769
Carbonel Series, 1153-1154
Cares Family Series, 1185-1188
Carey Family Series, 1324-1329
Carlos Series, 905-908
Carol Turner Series, 1264-1265
Caroline Series, 913-914

Carson St. Detectives, 1110-1113
Casey McKee Series, 290-291
Catfish Bend Series, 222-225
Cathie Stuart Series, 842-843
Changes Series, 401-403
Charley Moss Series, 704-706
Christophilos Series, 961-962
Cinda Hollister Series, 770-774
Cindy Series, 1006-1007
Clarence Series, 786-788

Danny Dunn Series, 1375-1386
David Series, 1417-1420
David Williams Series, 594-596
Derek Morgan Series, 1346-1347
Desmond Series, 128-131
Diane Series, 263-265
Dick Knox Series, 67-68
Dinny Gordon Series, 457-460
Dorrie Series, 324-332
Drew Rennie Series, 994-995
Drina Series, 23-31
Duncan McKenna Series, 333-334

Ellen Grae Series, 304-306
Emil Series, 828-829
Encyclopedia Brown Series, 1169-1176
Ethan Strong Series, 605-606

Five Yard Fuller Series, 1340-1343
Flambards Series, 1053-1055
Francie Series, 602-604
Freddy the Pig Series, 190-214
Fripsey Series, 269-272

Gaby Series, 122-127
Garland Family Series, 21-22
Ginnie Series, 1408-1416
Golden Stallion Series, 939-945
Gone-Away Series, 471-472
Great Brain Series, 530-533
Green Knowe Series, 172-176

Hackberry St. Series, 574-575
Hadley Family Series, 307-313
Hall Children Series, 777-779
Harald Sigurdson Series, 1232-1234

SERIES TITLE INDEX

Hardrada Trilogy Series, 1235-1237
Henry Huggins Series, 292-301
Henry Reed Series, 1106-1109
Homer the Turtle Series, 92-94
Horace Higby Series, 657-659
Hosteen Storm Series, 975-976
Hugo and Josephine Series, 599-601
Humphrey Series, 816-817

Island Stallion Series, 518-521

Janie Marshall Series, 1148-1152
Jase Landers Series, 915-916
Jase Mason Series, 725-728
Jean-Pierre Series, 558-561
Jenny Linsky Series, 69-81
Jim Beatty Series, 921-923
Joe Panther Series, 917-920
Jonathon Flower Series, 37-39
Jordon Family Series, 742-752
Joshua Cobb Series, 677-678

Kalena Series, 170-171
Kati Series, 826-827
Katie John Series, 234-236
Ken Holt Series, 475-492
Kent Barstow Series, 946-952
Kindness Club Series, 82-83
Kit Harris Series, 1070-1071
Krip Vorlund Series, 973-974

Lalu Series, 1177-1178
Larsson Family Series, 1243-1246
Lechow Family Series, 116-118
Leonard Family Series, 1398-1404
Libby Series, 1405-1407
Lincoln Series, 527-529
Little House Series, 1362-1370
Little Pear Series, 782-785
Lookout Club Series, 578-593

McBroom Series, 536-540
Mad Scientists Series, 188-189
Magnus Series, 1046-1050
Marco Series, 546-548
Marcy Series, 433-436

Marilda Series, 102-104
Maris Series, 953-954
Marriner Family Series, 789-791
Marty Series, 132-134
Mary Ellis Series, 968-969
Matthew Looney Series, 105-108
Meg Series, 733-738
Michael Glenn Series, 794-795
Miller Family Series, 322-323
Minnipins Series, 717-718
Miranda Welch Series, 1261-1263
Mishmash Series, 318-321
Miss Bianca Series, 1136-1141
Miss Pickerell Series, 887-894
Mrs. Coverlet Series, 963-965
Mrs. Pepperpot Series, 1093-1097
Mr. Bass Series, 237-241
Mr. Murdock Series, 689-690
Mr. Toast Series, 183-185
Mitchell Family Series, 1247-1249
Molly Stewart Series, 153-155
Molly-O and Pip Series, 314-315
Monroe Family Series, 109-112
Moomin Series, 709-716
Morgan Connor Series, 1193-1194
Mushroom Planet Series, 237-241

Nancy Kimball Series, 739-741
Narnia Series, 805-811
Neil Lambert Series, 1110-1113
Nomusa Series, 934-936
Nurse Matilda Series, 812-813

Oak St. Boys Club Series, 168-169
Ollie Series, 1058-1064
Orphelines Series, 248-251
Otto Series, 417-420

Paddington Series, 156-164
Parri MacDonald Series, 761-764
Patty and Ginger Series, 753-758
Pauline Series, 731-732
Persever Family Series, 963-965
Pierce Family Series, 493-495
Pippi Longstocking Series, 823-825
Pleasant Fieldmouse Series, 1259-1260
Prydain Series, 14-20
Pye Family Series, 500-501

SERIES TITLE INDEX

Rachel Series, 814-815
Ralph the Mouse Series, 302-303
Rhada Series, 567-569
Richards Family Series, 702-703
Robby Hoenig Series, 404-406
Rocky McCune Series, 844-860
Roger Tearle Series, 337-339
Ross Murdock Series, 981-982
Rugged Dozen Series, 375-376

Shann Lantee Series, 983-984
Shy Stegosaurus Series, 775-776
Space Cat Series, 1226-1229
Spaceship Series, 837-838, 1155-1158
Spotlight Club Series, 649-650
Stacy Belford Series, 1302-1309
Sugar Bradley Series, 759-760

Tammy Series, 84-87
Tatum Family Series, 252-258
Teddy Tibbetts Series, 723-724
Three Boys Series, 1-8

Thursday Series, 165-167
Timothy Penny Series, 473-474
Tizz Series, 135-148
Tobey Heydon Series, 423-428
Tod Moran Series, 1033-1045
Tom and Jennifer Series, 242-243
Tornado Jones Series, 396-398
Tough Enough Series, 252-258
Travis Fox Series, 979-980
Treegate Family Series, 1352-1356
Trick Series, 340-347
Twm Tybach Series, 1250-1251

Veronica Ganz Series, 1123-1125

Warner Family Series, 1348-1349
Wendy Brent Series, 387-390
Whitey the Cowboy Series, 1114-1120
Windy Foot Series, 552-555
Witch World Series, 989-993

Zip-Zip Series, 1131-1133

TITLE INDEX

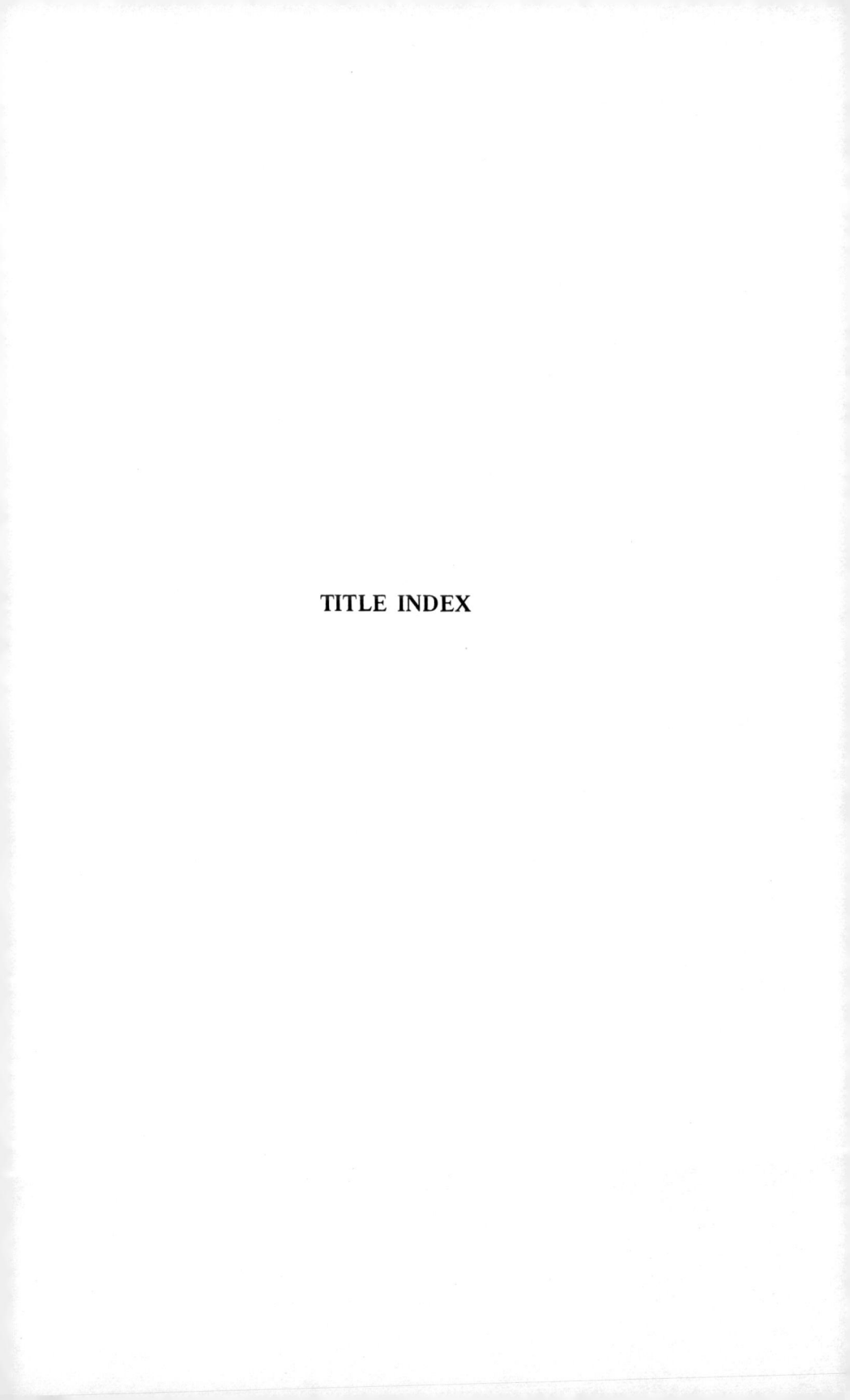

TITLE INDEX

Abandoned Mine Mystery, The, 1025
Adventure on Ghost River, 411
Adventure on Sunset Trail, 412
African Adventure, 1086
Again Christophilos, 962
Agaton Sax and the Diamond Thieves, 549
Agaton Sax and the Incredible Max Brothers, 551
Agaton Sax and the Scotland Yard Mystery, 550
Aggie, Maggie, and Tish, 496
Alfred Hitchcock and the Three Investigators in the Mystery of the Coughing Dragon, 1344
Alfred Hitchcock and the Three Investigators in the Mystery of the Fiery Eye, 61
Alfred Hitchcock and the Three Investigators in the Mystery of the Flaming Footprints, 244
Alfred Hitchcock and the Three Investigators in the Mystery of the Green Ghost, 58
Alfred Hitchcock and the Three Investigators in the Mystery of the Laughing Shadow, 50
Alfred Hitchcock and the Three Investigators in the Mystery of the Moaning Cave, 49
Alfred Hitchcock and the Three Investigators in the Mystery of the Nervous Lion, 1345
Alfred Hitchcock and the Three Investigators in the Mystery of the Screaming Clock, 63
Alfred Hitchcock and the Three Investigators in the Mystery of the Shrinking House, 52
Alfred Hitchcock and the Three Investigators in the Mystery of the Silver Spider, 62
Alfred Hitchcock and the Three Investigators in the Mystery of the Singing Serpent, 245
Alfred Hitchcock and the Three Investigators in the Mystery of the Stuttering Parrot, 56
Alfred Hitchcock and the Three Investigators in the Mystery of the Talking Skull, 64
Alfred Hitchcock and the Three Investigators in the Mystery of the Vanishing Treasure, 59
Alfred Hitchcock and the Three Investigators in the Mystery of the Whispering Mummy, 57
Alfred Hitchcock and the Three Investigators in the Secret of Skeleton Island, 60
Alfred Hitchcock and the Three Investigators in the Secret of Terror Castle, 55
Alfred Hitchcock and the Three Investigators in the Secret of the Crooked Cat, 51
All-of-a-Kind Family, 1212
All-of-a-Kind Family Downtown, 1215
All-of-a-Kind Family Uptown, 1214
Alley, The, 498
Alligator Case, The, 421
Allth, 1105
Almost April, 1142
Alvin Fernald, Foreign Trader, 662
Alvin Fernald, Mayor for a Day, 663
Alvin's Secret Code, 661
Amazon Adventure, 1081
Amy and Laura, 1128
Amy Moves In, 1126
Anchor Man, 705
Angel in Heavy Shoes, 1306
Anna, 36
Annie Pat and Eddie, 639
Appomattox Road, 1336
April Adventure, 1008
Ark, The, 116
Astonishing Stereoscope, The, 779
Aunt Vinnie's Invasion, 45
Aunt Vinnie's Victorious Six, 46
Automatic Strike, The, 850
Awful Name to Live Up To, An, 685
Azor, 361
Azor and the Blue-Eyed Cow, 362

"B" Is for Betsy, 624
Back to School with Betsy, 626
Backcourt Man, 656
Baffling Affair in the County Hospital, 390
Ballerina on Skates, 1143
Ballet Family, The, 21
Ballet for Drina, 23
Bandoleer, 121
Baseball Mystery, The, 1023
Baseball Trick, The, 344
Bases Loaded, 868
Basil and the Lost Colony, 1224
Basil and the Pygmy Cats, 1225
Basil of Baker Street, 1223
Battle at Bear Paw Gap, 1338
Battle for King's Mountain, The, 1331

TITLE INDEX

Battle of St. George Without, The, 903
Beanie, 252
Beany and the Beckoning Road, 1313
Beany Has a Secret Life, 1314
Beany Malone, 1311
Bear Called Paddington, A, 156
Bears Back in Business, The, 90
Beast Master, 975
Beatty of the Yankees, 922
Becky's Birthday, 1238
Becky's Christmas, 1239
Beethoven Medal, The, 1057
Beezus and Ramona, 297
Belling the Tiger, 1195
Beneath the Hill, 367
Best Birthday Party, The, 955
Best Friends, 95
Best Friends at School, 97
Best Friends in Summer, 96
Best of Friends, The, 82
Betsy and Billy, 625
Betsy and Mr. Kilpatrick, 643
Betsy and the Boys, 627
Betsy and the Circus, 633
Betsy's Busy Summer, 635
Betsy's Little Star, 680
Betsy's Winterhouse, 637
Beyond Hawaii, 1349
Beyond the Burning Lands, 283
Beyond the Pawpaw Trees, 215
Bicycle Mystery, 1296
Big Cat Mystery, The, 1021
Big Deal, 772
Big Ninth, The, 872
Big Splash, The, 720
Bigger Game, The, 845
Bill Bergson and the White Rose Rescue, 822
Bill Bergson Lives Dangerously, 821
Bill Bergson, Master Detective, 820
Birdy and the Group, 667
Birdy Jones, 666
Black Cauldron, The, 15
Black Hearts in Battersea, 10
Black Stallion, The, 504
Black Stallion and Flame, The, 514, 521
Black Stallion and Satan, The, 507
Black Stallion and the Girl, The, 517
Black Stallion Challenged, The, 515
Black Stallion Returns, The, 505
Black Stallion Revolts, The, 510
Black Stallion's Courage, The, 512

Black Stallion's Filly, The, 509
Black Stallion's Ghost, The, 516
Black Stallion's Mystery, The, 513
Black Stallion's Sulky Colt, The, 511
Black Tanker, The, 1040
Black Thumb Mystery, The, 477
Black Tiger, 1357
Black Tiger at Bonneville, 1360
Black Tiger at Indianapolis, 1361
Black Tiger at Le Mans, 1359
Blackbeard's Ghost, 1189
Blast-Off at 0300, 1271
Blood Bay Colt, The, 508
Blow a Wild Bugle for Catfish Bend, 225
Blue Bay Mystery, 1287
Blue Man, The, 1072
Blue Mystery, 114
Blueberry, 1129
Blueberry Summer, 1004
Bluffer, The, 876
Bob Bodden and the Good Ship "Rover," 1635
Bob Bodden and the Seagoing Farm, 1636
Book of Three, The, 14
Borrowed Treasure, 314
Borrowers, The, 996
Borrowers Afield, The, 997
Borrowers Afloat, The, 998
Borrowers Aloft, The, 999
Bowman of Crecy, 1329
Boxcar Children, The, 1282
Boy Alone, 1011
Boy Trouble, 425
Boy Upstairs, The, 1298
Boy Wanted, 754
Boyhood of Grace Jones, The, 781
Bread-and-Butter Indian, 316
Bread-and-Butter Journey, 317
Bright and Morning Star, The, 619
Bright Days, 269
Bright Star Falls, A, 1318
Bright Tomorrow, A, 751
Bristle Face, 915
Brogeen and the Bronze Lizard, 841
Brogeen and the Little Wind, 839
Brogeen Follows the Magic Tune, 840
Brother for the Orphelines, A, 249
Brumby, Come Home, 1032
Brumby the Wild White Stallion, 1031
Bud Baker, College Pitcher, 701
Bud Baker, High School Pitcher, 700

TITLE INDEX

Bud Baker, Racing Swimmer, 698
Bud Baker, T Quarterback, 697
Bud Plays Junior High Basketball, 696
Bud Plays Junior High Football, 695
Bud Plays Senior High Basketball, 699
Buffalo Horse, 278
Buffalo Kill, 276
Buffalo Robe, The, 277
Buffalo Trace, The, 452
Bully of Barkham St., The, 1192
Burnish Me Bright, 365
By the Shores of Silver Lake, 1366

Caboose Mystery, 1292
Cadet Attack, 1003
Cadet Command, 1002
Cadet Quarterback, 1001
Call Me Charley, 704
Camerons, Ahoy!, 441
Camerons at the Castle, 439
Camerons Calling, The, 440
Camerons on the Hills, 438
Camerons on the Train, 437
Cammie's Challenge, 896
Cammie's Choice, 895
Cammie's Cousin, 897
Canadian Summer, 1248
Cap for Mary Ellis, A, 968
Cape Cod Casket, 38
Captain of the "Araby," 1044
Captains of the City Streets, 80
Captive Coach, 844
Capture of the Golden Stallion, The, 939
Carbonel, The King of the Cats, 1153
Caroline and Her Kettle Named Maud, 913
Caroline and the Seven Little Words, 914
Case of the Diamond Eye, The, 1266
Case of the Fugitive Firebug, The, 338
Case of the Gone Goose, The, 337
Case of the Ticklish Tooth, The, 339
Castle of Llyr, The, 16
Castle on the Border, 118
Castors Away!, 226
Cat Club, The, 69
Cathie and the Paddy Boy, 843
Cathie Stuart, 842
Cathy and the Beautiful People, 1403
Cathy at the Crossroads, 502
Cathy Leonard Calling, 1400
Cathy Uncovers a Secret, 1404

Cathy's Little Sister, 1401
Cathy's Secret Kingdom, 503
Championship Quarterback, 926
Change for a Penny, 474
Charley Starts from Scratch, 706
Charlie and the Chocolate Factory, 370
Charlie and the Great Glass Elevator, 371
Charlotte Sometimes, 524
Children of Green Knowe, The, 172
Chris in Trouble, 1402
Christmas Dolls, The, 1425
Cinda, 770
Cindy's Sad and Happy Tree, 1007
Cindy's Snowdrops, 1006
City High Champs, 655
City High Five, 654
City of Gold and Lead, The, 280
Clarence Goes to Town, 787
Clarence the TV Dog, 786
Clarence Turns Sea Dog, 788
Clash on Catawba, 1332
Class Ring, 424
Clint Lane in Korea, 1103
Clubhouse, The, 906
Clue of the Black Cat, The, 125
Clue of the Coiled Cobra, The, 479
Clue of the Marked Claw, The, 478
Clue of the Phantom Car, The, 482
Clue of the Silver Scorpion, The, 490
Clues in the Woods, 1029
Cold Seas Beyond, The, 1144
Coll and His White Pig, 20
Collected Poems of Freddy the Pig, The, 214
Colonel Shepperton's Clock, 1240
Come Back, Wherever You Are, 1323
Comet in Moominland, 715
Community of Men, A, 722
Confusion—By Cupid, 744
Corner Back, The, 929
Cossacks, The, 100
Counterfeit Mystery, The, 1019
Country Cousin, 373
County Fair, 463
Cricket in Times Square, The, 1216
Cristy at Skippinghills, 688
Crocodile Adventure, 1092
Crow and the Castle, The, 1112
Crystal Mountain, 1121
Crystal Tree, The, 832
Cuckoo Tree, The, 12
Curious Calamity in Ward 8, 387

TITLE INDEX

Curious Clubhouse, The, 576
Curse of the Viking Grave, The, 958
Cutlass Island, 336

D.J.'s Worst Enemy, 220
Dagger, the Fish, and Casey McKee, The, 290
Dancing Garlands, The, 22
Danny Dunn and the Anti-Gravity Paint, 1375
Danny Dunn and the Automatic House, 1383
Danny Dunn and the Fossil Cave, 1380
Danny Dunn and the Heat Ray, 1381
Danny Dunn and the Homework Machine, 1377
Danny Dunn and the Smallifying Machine, 1385
Danny Dunn and the Swamp Monster, 1386
Danny Dunn and the Voice from Space, 1384
Danny Dunn and the Weather Machine, 1378
Danny Dunn on a Desert Island, 1376
Danny Dunn on the Ocean Floor, 1379
Danny Dunn, Time Traveler, 1382
Dark Treasure, 266
Date for Diane, A, 263
Daughter of Wolf House, 112
David's Campaign Buttons, 1420
David's Hundred Dollars, 1419
David's Railroad, 1417
Day and the Way We Met, The, 1194
Day It Rained Forever, The, 795
Day It Rained Sidneys, The, 1346
Day Jean-Pierre Joined the Circus, The, 561
Day Jean Pierre Was Pignapped, The, 559
Day Jean-Pierre Went Round the World, The, 560
Day the Guinea Pig Talked, The, 558
Day the Spaceship Landed, The, 837
Daybreakers, The, 368
Debbie of the Green Gate, 374
Defiant Agents, The, 980
Defiant Bride, The, 180
Depend on Katie John, 235
Desert Storm, 543
Desmond and Dog Friday, 131
Desmond and the Peppermint Ghost, 130

Desmond the Dog Detective, 129
Desmond's First Case, 128
Detectives in Togas, 1396
Devil's Children, The, 403
Devil's Hill, 274
Diamond in the Window, The, 777
Diamonds Are More Trouble, 349
Diamonds Are Trouble, 348
Diane's New Love, 264
Dinny Gordon, Freshman, 457
Dinny Gordon, Junior, 459
Dinny Gordon, Senior, 460
Dinny Gordon, Sophomore, 458
Disappearing Dog Trick, The, 342
Diving Adventure, 1091
Dr. Anger's Island, 217
Doctor's Boy, 43
Dog and a Half, A, 1373
Dog on Barkham St., A, 1191
Doll House Mystery, The, 707
Don't Call Me Katie Rose, 1302
Dorrie and the Birthday Eggs, 331
Dorrie and the Blue Witch, 325
Dorrie and the Goblin, 332
Dorrie and the Haunted House, 330
Dorrie and the Weather Box, 327
Dorrie and the Witch Doctor, 328
Dorrie and the Wizard's Spell, 329
Dorrie's Magic, 324
Dorrie's Play, 326
Double Date, 429
Double Feature, 430
Double Steal, The, 851
Double Wedding, 432
Drag Race Driver, 416
Dream for Susan, A, 745
Drina Dances Again, 26
Drina Dances in Exile, 25
Drina Dances in Italy, 28
Drina Dances in Madeira, 30
Drina Dances in New York, 27
Drina Dances in Paris, 29
Drina Dances in Switzerland, 31
Drina's Dancing Year, 24
Drums in my Heart, 792
Duncan's World, 333

Eagle Scout, 871
Eagle's Paradise, 219
Eddie and Gardenia, 631

TITLE INDEX

Eddie and His Big Deals, 634
Eddie and Louella, 638
Eddie and the Fire Engine, 629
Eddie Makes Music, 636
Eddie the Dogholder, 642
Eddie's Green Thumb, 641
Eddie's Happenings, 646
Eddie's Pay Dirt, 632
Edgar Allen, 966
Edge of Disaster, 615
Edge of the Cloud, The, 1054
Edie on the Warpath, 1188
Elephant Adventure, 1087
Ellen, 35
Ellen Grae, 304
Ellen Tebbits, 293
Emil in the Soup Tureen, 828
Emil's Pranks, 829
Emma in Winter, 523
Emma's Island, 66
Emmy and the Blue Door, 931
Emmy Keeps a Promise, 267
Empty House Mystery, The, 1018
Enchantress from the Stars, 469
Encounter Near Venus, 1350
Encyclopedia Brown and the Case of the Secret Pitch, 1170
Encyclopedia Brown, Boy Detective, 1169
Encyclopedia Brown Finds the Clues, 1171
Encyclopedia Brown Gets His Man, 1172
Encyclopedia Brown Keeps the Peace, 1174
Encyclopedia Brown Saves the Day, 1175
Encyclopedia Brown Solves Them All, 1173
Encyclopedia Brown Tracks Them Down, 1176
Enemies of the Secret Hide-Out, 1052
Enemy at Green Knowe, An, 176
Enemy Seas, The, 1146
Escape from France, 1325
Especially Humphrey, 816
Ethan Strong: Strike and Fight Back, 605
Ethan Strong: Watch by the Sea, 606
Euloowirree Walkabout, 721
Ever-Ready Eddie, 644
Exiles of the Stars, 974
Expedition Venus, 1275
Exploits of Moominpappa, The, 713
Extra Special, 757
Extra-Special Room, The, 674

Fabulous, 120
Fabulous Flying Bicycle, The, 408
Fabulous Year, The, 1005
Fairwater, 1104
Family Conspiracy, The, 1066
Family from One-End Street, The, 564
Family Grandstand, 186
Family Sabbatical, 187
Family Tower, The, 1371
Fanny, 34
Far in the Day, 366
Far Side of Evil, The, 470
Farmer Boy, 1364
Farthest Shore, The, 798
Fast Green Car, 230
February's Road, 1253
Fielder's Choice, 865
Finn Family Moomintroll, 712
Fire Cat, The, 81
Fireworks for Windy Foot, 555
First and Ten, 861
First Four Years, The, 1370
First Love Farewell, 468
First Love, True Love, 466
First of All, 769
First on the Moon, 1273
First Orchid for Pat, 467
First Semester, 1207
Five Dolls and the Duke, 289
Five Dolls and the Monkey, 288
Five Dolls and Their Friends, 286
Five Dolls in a House, 285
Five Dolls in the Snow, 287
Five-Man Break, The, 853
Five Yard Fuller, 1340
Five Yard Fuller and the Unlikely Knights, 1342
Five Yard Fuller of the New York Gnats, 1341
Five Yard Fuller's Mighty Model T, 1343
Five Yards to Glory, 848
Five's a Crowd, 768
Flambards, 1053
Flambards in Summer, 1055
Fly Away, Cinda, 771
Flying Tackle, 866
Foghorn, 1038
For Each Other, 766
For the King, 1326
Forever and Ever, 767
Francie, 602

TITLE INDEX

Francie Again, 603
Francie Comes Home, 604
Freddy and Freginald, 207
Freddy and Mr. Camphor, 196
Freddy and Simon the Dictator, 211
Freddy and the Baseball Team from Mars, 210
Freddy and the Bean Home News, 195
Freddy and the Dragon, 213
Freddy and the Flying Saucer Plans, 212
Freddy and the Ignoramus, 193
Freddy and the Men from Mars, 209
Freddy and the Perilous Adventure, 194
Freddy and the Pied Piper, 198
Freddy and the Popinjay, 197
Freddy and the Space Ship, 208
Freddy Goes Camping, 200
Freddy Goes to Florida, 202
Freddy Goes to the North Pole, 204
Freddy Plays Football, 201
Freddy Rides Again, 205
Freddy the Cowboy, 203
Freddy the Detective, 190
Freddy the Magician, 199
Freddy the Pilot, 206
Freddy the Politician, 191
Freddy's Cousin Weedly, 192
Frederika's Children, 1299
Friday's Child, 743
Friday's Tunnel, 1252
Friendly Gables, 1249
Fripsey Fun, 271
Fripsey Summer, 270
Further Adventures of the Family from One-End Street, The, 565

Galactic Derelict, 979
Gammage Cup, The, 717
Gates of Eden, The, 900
Gateway to the Sun, 793
Ghost Battalion, 1334
Ghost Boat, The, 703
Ghost of Dagger Bay, The, 218
Ghosts Who Went to School, 1179
Gift of Gold, 229
Ginger Lee: War Nurse, 381
Ginger Pye, 500
Gingerbread, 1130
Ginnie and Geneva, 1408
Ginnie and Her Juniors, 1413

Ginnie and the Cooking Contest, 1414
Ginnie and the Mystery Cat, 1416
Ginnie and the Mystery Doll, 1412
Ginnie and the Mystery House, 1411
Ginnie and the New Girl, 1410
Ginnie and the Wedding Bells, 1415
Ginnie Joins In, 1409
Glitter-Eyed Wouser, The, 791
Glory Tent, The, 99
Go-Ahead Runner, The, 884
Goal in the Sky, 670
Golden Name Day, The, 830
Golden Stallion and the Mysterious Feud, The, 945
Golden Stallion and the Wolf Dog, The, 942
Golden Stallion to the Rescue, The, 941
Golden Stallion's Adventure at Redstone, The, 944
Golden Stallion's Revenge, The, 940
Golden Stallion's Victory, The, 943
Gone-Away Lake, 471
Good Charlotte, 1427
Good Day Mice, The, 1426
Good Land, The, 495
Good Light, The, 152
Good Luck to the Rider, 1065
Goodbye, Dove Square, 904
Gorilla Adventure, 1090
Grand Prix Germany, 68
Grand Prix Monaco, 67
Grand Slam Homer, 869
Grandmother Oma, 729
Grange at High Force, The, 1241
Grass Was That High, The, 1070
Great Brain, The, 530
Great Brain at the Academy, The, 533
Great Rebellion, The, 1196
Greenhouse Mystery, The, 1027
Grover, 306
Guns in the Heather, 37

Hairy Horror Trick, The, 346
Hakon of Rogen's Saga, 620
Half Magic, 446
Half Sisters, The, 246
Half-Time Gypsy, The, 1251
Hannibal and the Bears, 89
Happy Birthday, Dear Beany, 1316
Happy Little Family, 259
Happy Orpheline, The, 248

TITLE INDEX

Harriet the Spy, 534
Hatching of Joshua Cobb, The, 677
Hateful Plateful Trick, The, 347
Haunted House, 1030
Haunted Reef, The, 355
Hawk, The, 1328
Healing Blade, The, 352
Heart of Danger, 1042
Heartsease, 402
Hello, My Love, Goodbye, 1308
Henchmans at Home, The, 227
Henry and Beezus, 294
Henry and Ribsy, 296
Henry and the Clubhouse, 299
Henry and the Paper Route, 298
Henry Huggins, 292
Henry Reed, Inc., 1106
Henry Reed's Babysitting Service, 1108
Henry Reed's Big Show, 1109
Henry Reed's Journey, 1107
Herbert, 1390
Herbert Again, 1391
Herbert's Homework, 1393
Herbert's Space Trip, 1394
Herbert's Stilts, 1395
Here Comes the Bus, 647
Here Comes Thursday, 165
Here's Marny, 752
Hi, Neighbor, 760
Hickory Hill, 464
Hidden Harbor, 1068
Hidden Trail, 728
Hiding Place, The, 909
High Heels for Jennifer, 1166
High House, The, 65
High King, The, 18
High Water at Catfish Bend, 222
Highroad to Adventure, 1039
Hi-Jinks Joins the Bears, 91
Holiday at the Dew Drop Inn, A One-End Story, 566
Holiday on Wheels, 1418
Home Run Harvest, 854
Homer Goes to Stratford, 94
Homer Sees the Queen, 93
Homer the Tortoise, 92
Honest Dollar, The, 1148
Honestly, Katie John, 236
Horace Higby and the Field Goal Formula, 657
Horace Higby and the Scientific Pitch, 658
Horace Higby, Coxswain of the Crew, 659

Horse and His Boy, The, 809
Horse in the Camel Suit, The, 422
Horse Without a Head, The, 122
Hostess in the Sky, 671
Hostile Beaches, The, 1145
Hot Corner, The, 846
Hotel Cat, The, 79
House at World's End, The, 399
Houseboat Mystery, 1293
How Bright the Dawn, 1265
How Juan Got Home, 908
How Long Is Always?, 1307
How the Brothers Joined the Cat Club, 75
Hubble's Bubble, 683
Hubbles' Treasure Hunt, The, 684
Hugo, 601
Hugo and Josephine, 600
Humphrey on the Town, 817
Hundred and One Dalmations, The, 1159
Hunger for Racing, 413
Hunt Down the Prize, 954
Hurricane Weather, 1037

I Met a Boy I Used to Know, 1305
Incomplete Pitcher, 860
Ink Bottle Club, The, 1167
Ink Bottle Club Abroad, 1168
Introducing Parri, 761
Iron Arm of Michael Glenn, The, 794
Isfendiar and the Bears of Mazandaran, 1080
Isfendiar and the Wild Donkeys, 1079
Island Stallion, The, 518
Island Stallion Races, The, 520
Island Stallion's Fury, The, 519
Island Summer, 1010
Ismo, 1254

Jackknife for a Penny, 473
Jamberoo Road, 1182
Jan and the Wild Horse, 391
Java Wreckmen, The, 357
Jennifer Dances, 1165
Jennifer Gift, The, 1162
Jennifer is Eleven, 1164
Jennifer Prize, The, 1163
Jennifer Wish, The, 1161
Jenny, 693
Jenny Goes to Sea, 77

TITLE INDEX

Jenny the Fire Maker, 597
Jenny's Adopted Brothers, 74
Jenny's Bedside Book, 78
Jenny's Birthday Book, 76
Jenny's First Party, 71
Jenny's Moonlight Adventure, 72
Jet Pilot, 803
Jet Pilot Overseas, 804
Jinx Ship, The, 1034
John Treegate's Musket, 1352
Josephine, 599
Journey of the Eldest Son, The, 557
Journey to Jupiter, 1278
Journey to Untor, 1351
Judgement on Janus, 987
Just Jennifer, 742

Kalena, 170
Kalena and Sana, 171
Kate, 836
Kati in Italy, 826
Kati in Paris, 827
Katia, 32
Katie and Nan, 691
Katie and Nan Go to Sea, 692
Katie John, 234
Kent Barstow Aboard the Dyna Soar, 952
Kent Barstow and the Commando Flight, 950
Kent Barstow on a B-70 Mission, 951
Kent Barstow, Spaceman, 949
Kent Barstow, Special Agent, 946
Key Out of Time, 982
Key to the Treasure, 1028
Keys for Signe, 48
Kim Fashions a Career, 1134
Kim in Style, 1135
Kingdom of Carbonel, The, 1154
Kittens and the Cardinals, The, 83
Knee Deep in Thunder, 953
Knight's Castle, 447
Knock at the Door, Emmy, 930

Lady Ellen Grae, 305
Lark in the Morn, The, 1256
Lark on the Wing, The, 1257
Lark Shall Sing, The, 232
Last Battle, The, 811
Last Out, The, 923

Last Put-Out, The, 873
Last Viking, The, 1236
Laura's Luck, 1127
Leap into Danger, 614
Leave It to Beany, 1312
Leave It to the Fripseys, 272
Legion Tourney, 864
Lemon and a Star, A, 1185
Lemonade Trick, The, 340
Leopard's Prey, 1356
Lesson for Janie, A, 1149
Letters to Pauline, 732
Libby Looks for a Spy, 1406
Libby's Uninvited Guest, 1407
Light a Single Candle, 228
Lighthouse Mystery, The, 1289
Lilies of the Field, The, 98
Lillie of Watts: A Birthday Discovery, 1269
Lillie of Watts Takes a Giant Step, 1270
Limerick Trick, The, 343
Linebacker, The, 928
Lion Adventure, 1089
Lion, the Witch and the Wardrobe, The, 805
Lisa Bright and Dark, 967
Little Eddie, 628
Little House in the Big Woods, 1362
Little House on the Prairie, 1363
Little O, 1245
Little Old Mrs. Pepperpot, 1093
Little Pear, 782
Little Pear and His Friends, 783
Little Pear and the Rabbits, 784
Little Plum, 573
Little Silver House, The, 831
Little Sister Tai-Mi, 182
Little Town on the Prairie, 1368
Locked Safe Mystery, The, 1015
Long Pitcher, The, 857
Long Secret, The, 535
Long Winter, The, 1367
Look Alive, Libby, 1405
Look Through My Window, 835
Lord of Thunder, 976
Losing Game, The, 462
Lost in the Barrens, 957
Louie's Lot, 668
Louie's SOS, 669
Love Is Forever, 111
Love Taps Gently, 746
Love to Spark, 774

TITLE INDEX

Lucy, 1198
Lucy Runs Away, 1199
Luvvy and the Girls, 247

McBroom and the Big Wind, 537
McBroom Tells the Truth, 536
McBroom's Ear, 538
McBroom's Ghost, 539
McBroom's Zoo, 540
Mad Scientists' Club, The, 188
Madcap Mystery, 42
Magic by the Lake, 448
Magic Island, 268
Magic Maker, The, 1250
Magic or Not?, 444
Magician's Nephew, The, 810
Magnificent Jalopy, The, 1230
Magnus and the Ship's Mascot, 1050
Magnus and the Squirrel, 1046
Magnus and the Wagon Horse, 1047
Magnus in Danger, 1049
Magnus in the Harbor, 1048
Mailbox Trick, The, 341
Majesty of Grace, The, 780
Make a Wish for Me, 1315
Making of Joshua Cobb, The, 678
Malkin's Mountain, 1389
Man for Marcy, A, 435
Man in Motion, 877
Man with a Sword, 1235
Manila Menfish, The, 358
Maple Sugar for Windy Foot, 554
Marco and That Curious Cat, 548
Marco and the Sleuth Hound, 547
Marco and the Tiger, 546
Marcy Catches Up, 434
Marilda and the Bird of Time, 104
Marilda and the Witness Tree, 103
Marilda's House, 102
Marsh King, The, 676
Marty, 132
Marty Goes to Hollywood, 133
Marty on the Campus, 134
Marv, 1125
Marvelous Inventions of Alvin Fernald, The, 660
Mary Ellis, Student Nurse, 969
Master of Morgana, 899
Matter of Pride, A, 1150
Matthew Looney and the Space Pirates, 108

Matthew Looney in the Outback, 107
Matthew Looney's Invasion of the Earth, 106
Matthew Looney's Voyage to the Earth, 105
Me and Caleb, 932
Me and Caleb Again, 933
Me and My Little Brain, 532
Meet the Austins, 800
Meet the Malones, 1310
Meg and Melissa, 736
Meg of Heron's Neck, 733
Meg's Mysterious Island, 735
Menace from the Moon, 1272
Merry Christmas from Betsy, 645
Mexican Road Race, 1358
Midshipman Quinn, 1200
Midshipman Quinn and Denise the Spy, 1202
Mike's Mystery, 1286
Mill Creek Irregulars, The, 394
Mine for Keeps, 833
Mishmash, 318
Mishmash and the Sauerkraut Mystery, 320
Mishmash and the Substitute Teacher, 319
Mishmash and Uncle Looey, 321
Miss Bianca, 1137
Miss Bianca in the Antarctic, 1141
Miss Bianca in the Orient, 1140
Miss Bianca in the Salt Mines, 1139
Miss Cathy Leonard, 1399
Miss Grimsbee Is a Witch, 1300
Miss Grimsbee Takes a Vacation, 1301
Miss Happiness and Miss Flower, 572
Miss Know-It-All, 1424
Miss Pickerell and the Geiger Counter, 888
Miss Pickerell and the Weather Satellite, 894
Miss Pickerell Goes on a Dig, 892
Miss Pickerell Goes to Mars, 887
Miss Pickerell Goes to the Arctic, 890
Miss Pickerell Goes Undersea, 889
Miss Pickerell Harvests the Sea, 893
Miss Pickerell on the Moon, 891
Miss Rivers and Miss Bridges, 1209
Missile Away, 947
Missing Witness Mystery, The, 1022
Mission Intruder, 948
Mission to Mercury, 1277
Mission to the Moon, 378
Mrs. Coverlet's Detectives, 965
Mrs. Coverlet's Magicians, 964

TITLE INDEX

Mrs. Pepperpot Again, 1094
Mrs. Pepperpot in the Magic Wood, 1096
Mrs. Pepperpot to the Rescue, 1095
Mrs. Pepperpot's Outing, 1097
Mist on the Mountain, 542
Mr. Bass's Planetoid, 239
Mr. Dawson Had a Farm, 1421
Mr. Dawson Had a Lamb, 1423
Mr. Dawson Had an Elephant, 1422
Mr. Midshipman Murdock and the Barbary Pirates, 689
Mr. Murdock Takes Command, 690
Mr. Toast and the Secret of Gold Hill, 185
Mr. Toast and the Woolly Mammoth, 184
Misty of Chincoteague, 651
Mitchells, The, 1247
Mohawk Valley, 1324
Mohole Menace, The, 1280
Money Machine, The, 1113
Moominland Midwinter, 710
Moominpappa at Sea, 714
Moominsummer Madness, 709
Moominvalley in November, 716
Moon by Night, The, 801
Moon in the Cloud, The, 617
Moon of Gomrath, The, 563
Moon of Three Rings, The, 973
Moon Tenders, The, 393
More About Little Pear, 785
More About Paddington, 158
More Adventures of the Great Brain, 531
More All-of-a-Kind Family, 1213
More Fun with Herbert, 1392
More the Merrier, The, 1317
Motoring Millers, The, 323
Mountain Stallion, 544
Mountain Top Mystery, 1290
Mouse and the Motorcycle, The, 302
Mule on the Expressway, The, 127
Museum House Ghosts, The, 1180
My Davy, 764
My Kingdom for a Grave, 1076
My World's the Stage, 1263
Myself and I, 748
Mysterious Christmas Shell, The, 243
Mysterious Discovery in Ward K, 389
Mysterious Machine, The, 407
Mysterious Schoolmaster, The, 40
Mystery at Bear Paw Gap, The, 1337
Mystery at Fearsome Lake, The, 587
Mystery at Ghost Lodge, The, 591

Mystery at Moccasin Bend, The, 581
Mystery at Plum Nelly, The, 586
Mystery at Rock City, The, 588
Mystery at Shingle Rock, The, 578
Mystery at the Deserted Mill, The, 583
Mystery at the Doll Hospital, The, 679
Mystery at the Echoing Cave, The, 593
Mystery at the Haunted House, The, 585
Mystery at the Indian Hide-Out, The, 582
Mystery at the Mountain Face, The, 579
Mystery at the Shuttered Hotel, The, 580
Mystery at the Snowed-In Cabin, The, 589
Mystery at the Weird Ruins, The, 592
Mystery for Meg, A, 734
Mystery for Mr. Bass, A, 240
Mystery in the Sand, 1297
Mystery in the Square Tower, The, 680
Mystery of Burnt Hill, The, 1110
Mystery of Castle Croome, The, 153
Mystery of Island Keep, The, 154
Mystery of Rainbow Gulch, The, 1024
Mystery of Saint Salgue, The, 124
Mystery of the Auction Trunk, The, 681
Mystery of the Blue Admiral, The, 308
Mystery of the Dancing Skeleton, The, 590
Mystery of the Fat Cat, The, 168
Mystery of the Galloping Horse, The, 483
Mystery of the Gallows Cliff, The, 489
Mystery of the Green Flame, The, 484
Mystery of the Grinning Tiger, The, 485
Mystery of the Invisible Enemy, The, 488
Mystery of the Iron Box, The, 481
Mystery of the Jade Green Cadillac, The, 310
Mystery of the Lost Tower Treasure, The, 311
Mystery of the Midnight Smugglers, The, 313
Mystery of the Missing Suitcase, The, 650
Mystery of the Plumed Serpent, The, 491
Mystery of the Roman Ransom, The, 1397
Mystery of the Scarlet Daffodil, The, 307
Mystery of the Shattered Glass, The, 487
Mystery of the Silver Tag, The, 649
Mystery of the Singing Strings, The, 312
Mystery of the Sultan's Scimitar, The, 492
Mystery of the Vanishing Magician, The, 486
Mystery of the Vanishing Stamp, The, 584
Mystery of the Witch Who Wouldn't, The, 1074

TITLE INDEX

Mystery of the Wooden Indian, The, 682
Mystery on Rainbow Island, The, 309
Mystery on Telegraph Hill, 1045
Mystery Ranch, 1285

Namesake, The, 675
Nancy Kimball, Nurse's Aide, 739
Navigator of Rhada, The, 568
Neptune One Is Missing, 1281
New Adventures of the Mad Scientists' Club, The, 189
New and Different Summer, A, 1304
New Birth of Freedom, 456
New Horizons, 1151
Nicholas Carey, 1327
Night Boat, 1041
Nightbirds on Nantucket, 11
Nitty Gritty, The, 169
No Place for Heroes, 859
Nomusa and the New Magic, 936
North Town, 595
Nose for Trouble, A, 725
Nothing Special, The, 1231
Now That I'm Sixteen, 354
Number 5 Hackberry Street, 574
Nurse in Training, 740
Nurse Matilda, 812
Nurse Matilda Goes to Town, 813

Oh, Sarah, 959
Old Sam and the Horse Thieves, 1211
Old Sam, Thoroughbred Trotter, 1210
Old Yeller, 570
Ollie, the Backward Forward, 1062
Ollie's Team and the Alley Cats, 1063
Ollie's Team and the Baseball Computer, 1058
Ollie's Team and the Basketball Computer, 1060
Ollie's Team and the Football Computer, 1059
Ollie's Team and the 200 Pound Problem, 1064
Ollie's Team Plays Biddy Baseball, 1061
On Her Own, 758
On the Banks of Plum Creek, 1365
Once a Slugger, 880
One O'Clock Hitter, 874
One of the Crowd, 428

Only Horse for Jan, The, 392
Operation Destruct, 970
Operation Manhunt, 971
Operation Neptune, 972
Orange October, 694
Ordeal in Otherwhere, 984
Orphelines in the Enchanted Castle, The, 251
Other Side of the Tunnel, The, 719
Otis Spofford, 295
Otto and the Magic Potatoes, 420
Otto at Sea, 417
Otto in Africa, 419
Otto in Texas, 418
Out of the Wilderness, 453
Outpost on the Moon, 1274
Over the Sea's Edge, 369
Owl Hoots Twice at Catfish Bend, The, 224

Paddington Abroad, 164
Paddington at Large, 159
Paddington at Work, 161
Paddington Goes to Town, 162
Paddington Helps Out, 157
Paddington Marches On, 160
Paddington Takes the Air, 163
Pagan the Black, 119
Paleface Redskins, The, 702
Pam Wilson: Registered Nurse, 384
Path Above the Pines, The, 1122
Pauline and the Prince in the Wind, 731
Pavilion, The, 1258
Peddler's Summer, 541
Peep-Larssons Go Sailing, The, 1246
Penderel Puzzle, The, 912
Pennington's Last Term, 1056
Penny and Pam: Nurse and Cadet, 383
Penny Marsh and Ginger Lee: Wartime Nurses, 382
Penny Marsh Finds Adventure, 385
Penny Marsh: Public Health Nurse, 379
Penny Marsh, R.N.: Director of Nurses, 386
Penny Marsh: Supervisor, 380
Perilous Wings, 616
Pet for the Orphelines, A, 250
Peter and Veronica, 1124
Peter Treegate's War, 1353
Phantom Shortstop, The, 855
Phoebe Snow, 607
Pick a New Dream, 1320

TITLE INDEX

Pilgrim Kate, 372
Pinkertons Ride Again, The, 395
Pinky Pye, 501
Pippi Goes on Board, 824
Pippi in the South Seas, 825
Pippi Longstocking, 823
Planet Poachers, The, 818
Play for One, The, 852
Pleasant Fieldmouse, 1259
Please Stand Clear of the Apache Arrows, 1347
Pool of Fire, The, 281
Poor Stainless, 1000
Popular Crowed, The, 461
Practically Seventeen, 423
Precious Days, The, 765
Prince Caspian, 806
Prince in Waiting, The, 282
Pringle and the Lavendar Goat, 364
Private Eyes, 724
Project: Genius, 622
Project: Scoop, 623
Promise of the Rose, The, 179
Proud Champions, 847
Pysen, 1244

Quarterback, The, 925
Queen's Blessing, The, 1077
Question of Harmony, A, 1183
Question of the Painted Cave, The, 911
Quick Kid, 870
Quinn at Trafalgar, 1203
Quinn of the "Fury," 1201

Rachel, 814
Rachel and Herman, 815
Racing to Glory, 414
Rain Comes to Yamboorah, 1013
Rambling Halfback, 867
Ramona the Pest, 301
Ready or Not, 1193
Real Thing, The, 426
Really Miss Hillsbro, 673
Rebel of Rhada, The, 567
Rebel Spurs, 995
Rebel with a Glove, 878
Receiver, The, 927
Renfroe's Christmas, 221
Rescuers, The, 1136

Return to Gone-Away, 472
Return to Hackberry Street, 575
Return to Racing, 231
Ribbon of Fire, 901
Ribsy, 300
Riddle of the Stone Elephant, The, 476
Ride for Jenny, A, 598
Ride, Proud Rebel, 994
Ride, Rebels, 1335
Rifles at Ramsour's Mill, 1330
Right-End Option, The, 882
River at Green Knowe, The, 174
Road to Agra, The, 1177
Road to Miklagard, The, 1233
Roan Colt, The, 1012
Roaring 40, The, 275
Robber Ghost, The, 41
Rookie, The, 924
Room for Cathy, A, 1398
Rough Stuff, 881
Round Trip Spaceship, 1158
Rowan Farm, 117
Rugged Dozen, The, 375
Rugged Dozen Abroad, The, 376
Runaway Pony, Runaway Dog, 258
Runaway Ralph, 303

"S. S. Shamrock" Mystery, The, 1026
Safari Adventure, 1088
Salvage Diver, 919
Sanguman, The, 360
Sarah Hastings, 960
Saturday Gang, The, 723
Saucepan Journey, The, 1243
Savage Sam, 571
Save the Khan, 101
Scarecrow Mystery, The, 1020
School for Cats, The, 70
Schoolhouse in the Woods, The, 260
Schoolhouse Mystery, 1291
Schoolroom in the Parlor, 262
Sea Ape, The, 359
Sea Captain from Salem, 1354
Sea Pup, 149
Sea Pup Again, 150
Sea Robbers, The, 356
Sea Star, 652
Search for a Golden Bird, The, 178
Seawind from Hawaii, 1348
Second Lieutenant Clint Lane, 1102

TITLE INDEX

Second Semester, 1207
Second Year Nurse, 741
Secret Castle, 315
Secret Hide-Out, The, 1051
Secret of Hangman's Inn, The, 480
Secret of Red Skull, The, 1190
Secret of Skeleton Island, The, 475
Secret of Thunder Mountain, The, 1014
Secret Spenders, The, 665
Secret Under Antarctica, 405
Secret Under the Caribbean, 406
Secret Under the Sea, 404
Secret Winners, The, 664
Seminole Trail, The, 443
Senior Hostess, 672
Senior Prom, 436
Seven Grandmothers, 935
Seven in Front, 885
Seven Stars for Catfish Bend, 223
Seven Sunflower Seeds, 1255
Shadow on the Sun, The, 618
Shanghai Passage, 1035
Ship Without a Crew, The, 1036
Shoe Shop Bears, The, 88
Shooting Star, 113
Shortstop, The, 921
Showboat Summer, 431
Shy Stegosaurus of Cricket Creek, The, 775
Shy Stegosaurus of Indian Springs, The, 776
Sierra Ranger, 1221
Silver Chair, The, 808
Silver Nutmeg, The, 216
Sinbad and Me, 1073
Singing Trees Mystery, The, 1017
Siri the Conquistador, 1197
Six Impossible Things, 233
Six Voyages of Pleasant Fieldmouse, The, 1260
Ski Ranger, 1222
Skin Diver, 918
Sky Diver, 920
Slave's Tale, A, 621
Sleigh Bells for Windy Foot, 553
Sly One, The, 39
Snowbound Mystery, 1249
Snowbound with Betsy, 640
So Near the Heart, 1262
Something Borrowed, Something Blue, 1322
Sometimes a Stranger, 1309

Son of the Black Stallion, 506
Song in Their Hearts, A, 747
Song of the Empty Bottles, 937
Song of the Smoggy Stars, 938
Sorceress of the Witch World, 993
Sound of Trumpets, A, 902
Sounder, 53
Sour Land, 54
South Fork Rangers, The, 1333
South Sea Adventure, 1082
South Town, 594
Space Ark, The, 819
Space Cat, 1226
Space Cat and the Kittens, 1229
Space Cat Meets Mars, 1228
Space Cat Visits Venus, 1227
Spaceship Returns, The, 838
Spaceship Returns to the Apple Tree, The, 1156
Spaceship to Saturn, 1279
Spaceship Under the Apple Tree, The, 1155
Spanish Gold and Casey McKee, 291
Specter of Bear Paw Gap, The, 1339
Spring Begins in March, 834
Spring Fever, 755
Sputters, 916
Stagestruck Parri, 763
Stand Up, Lucy, 608
Star Born, 986
Star-Crossed Stallion, 450
Star-Crossed Stallion's Big Chance, 451
Star Island, 609
Star Island Again, 610
Star Reporter Mystery, The, 1016
Starkahn of Rhada, 569
Starlight Barking, The, 1160
Starmaker, The, 862
Stars Are Ours, The, 985
Stars for Cristy, 687
Stars Grow Pale, The, 151
Stars Hang High, The, 749
Steam on the Line, 1242
Step to the Stars, 377
Stolen Seasons, The, 409
Storm Over Skye, 898
Storm Over Wales, 155
Storm Over Warlock, 983
Stormy, Misty's Foal, 653
Stowaway to the Mushroom Planet, 238
Strange Disappearance from Ward 2, 388

TITLE INDEX

Strange Disappearance of Mr. Toast, The, 183
Stranger at Green Knowe, A, 175
Stranger in the Backfield, 875
Street Musician, The, 123
Street of the Flower Boxes, The, 905
Struggle at Soltuna, 44
Summer at World's End, 400
Summer Birds, The, 522
Summer Madness, 756
Surprise Island, 1283, 1374
Swamp Chief, 917
Sweet As Sugar, 759
Sweet Sixteen, 465
Swing in the Summerhouse, The, 778
Switherby Pilgrims, The, 1181
Sword of the Spirits, The, 284
Swords from the North, 1237

Taffy and Melissa Molasses, 648
Tales from Moomin Valley, 711
Tales of Christophilos, 961
Tall at the Plate, 886
Tamarlane, 545
Tammy Camps in the Rocky Mountains, 87
Tammy Camps Out, 84
Tammy Climbs Pyramid Mountain, 85
Tammy Goes Canoeing, 86
Tammy Out of Time, 1204
Tammy Tell Me True, 1205
Taran Wanderer, 17
Tarry Awhile, 1321
Tattooed Man, The, 1033
Ten O'Clock Club, The, 1428
Terrible Churnadryne, The, 242
Terrible, Horrible Edie, 1187
Terror by Satellite, 1276
That's My Girl, 762
There Is a Happy Land, 47
These Happy Golden Years, 1369
Thirteenth Stone, The, 177
Thirty-one Brothers and Sisters, 934
This Snake Is Good, 334
Those Miller Girls!, 322
Threat to the Barkers, 1067
Three Against the Witch World, 991
Three Boys and a Helicopter, 6
Three Boys and a Lighthouse, 1
Three Boys and a Mine, 4
Three Boys and a Train, 5

Three Boys and a Tugboat, 3
Three Boys and H_2O, 8
Three Boys and Space, 7
Three Boys and the Remarkable Cow, 2
Three Brothers of Ur, The, 556
Three Lives for the Czar, 1075
Three Red Flares, 410
Three Rivers South, 454
Three-Seated Spaceship, 1157
Three Stars for Star Island, 611
Three Stuffed Owls, 1111
Three Toymakers, The, 1388
Three-Two Pitch, The, 863
Three Who Met, 353
Throwaway Catcher, The, 883
Thursday Ahoy!, 167
Thursday Rides Again, 166
Tiger in the Bush, 273
Time and Mr. Bass, 241
Time Garden, The, 449
Time to Love, A, 115
Time Traders, The, 981
Tina and the Latchkey Child, 1009
Tinker's Castle, 910
Tizz, 135
Tizz and Company, 138
Tizz at the Fiesta, 147
Tizz at the Stampede, 146
Tizz in Cactus Country, 142
Tizz in Texas, 143
Tizz in the Canadian Rockies, 145
Tizz Is a Cow Pony, 140
Tizz on a Horse Farm, 141
Tizz on a Pack Trip, 139
Tizz on a Trail Ride, 144
Tizz Plays Santa Claus, 137
Tizz South of the Border, 148
Tizz Takes a Trip, 136
To Kill a King, 1078
To Paris and Love, 613
Tombs of Atuan, The, 797
Too Late to Quit, 879
Too Many Forwards, 849
Toppling Towers, The, 1372
Tor and Azor, 363
Tornado Jones, 396
Tornado Jones on Sentinal Mountain, 397
Tornado's Big Year, 398
Torpedoes Away!, 1147
Totem Casts a Shadow, The, 110
Tough Enough, 253

TITLE INDEX

Tough Enough and Sassy, 256
Tough Enough's Indians, 257
Tough Enough's Pony, 255
Tough Enough's Trip, 254
Toujours Diane, 265
Toymaker's Daughter, The, 1387
Toyshop Mystery, The, 708
Trailing Trouble, 726
Trash Pile Treasure, The, 577
Traveling With Oma, 730
Treasure of Green Knowe, The, 173
Treasure of the High Country, 790
Treasure on Heron's Neck, 738
Tree House Island, 335
Tree House Mystery, 1295
Treegate's Raiders, 1355
Trina Finds a Brother, 181
Triple Trouble, 773
Trouble on Heron's Neck, 737
Truckload of Rice, A, 126
Truthful Harp, The, 19
Tucker's Countryside, 1217
Tunnel of Hugsy Goode, The, 499
Turnabout Trick, The 345
Turret, The, 1138
Twelve-Cylinder Screamer, The, 415
Twenty-four Days Before Christmas, The, 799
Two in the Wilderness, 1218
Two-One Attack, The, 856

Uncharted Stars, 978
Underwater Adventure, 1083
Up and Down the River, 261

Valerie Valentine Is Missing, 1268
Veronica Ganz, 1123
Victory on Janus, 988
Viking's Dawn, 1232
Viking's Sunset, 1234
Visitor from the Sea, 1152
Volcano Adventure, 1084
Voyage of the "Dawn Treader," The, 807

Wait for Marcy, 433
War Chant, 442
Warlock of the Witch World, 992
Watch for a Tall White Sail, 109

Weathermonger, The, 401
Web of the Witch World, 990
Wedding Bells, 750
Wedding in the Family, 427
Weirdstone, The, 562
Welcome, Stranger, 1319
Well-Wishers, The, 445
We're Going Steady, 753
West Point First Classman, 1101
West Point Plebe, 1098
West Point Second Classman, 1100
West Point Yearling, 1099
Whale Adventure, 1085
What Happened to Candy Carmichael?, 1267
What's New, Lincoln?, 528
What's the Prize, Lincoln?, 529
When Carlos Closed the Street, 907
When Jenny Lost Her Scarf, 73
When Love Speaks, 1261
Where Is My Heart, 1264
Where's Aggie?, 497
While Mrs. Coverlet Was Away, 963
Whirl of Fashion, 612
Whisper of Glocken, The, 718
Whispering Mountain, The, 13
White Bungalow, The, 1178
White Calf, The, 525
White Cockade, The, 350
White in the Moon, 1184
White Mountains, The, 279
White Peril, The, 526
Whitey and the Blizzard, 1114
Whitey and the Colt Killer, 1119
Whitey and the Wild Horse, 1117
Whitey Ropes and Rides, 1116
Whitey Takes a Trip, 1115
Whitey's First Roundup, 1118
Whitey's New Saddle, 1120
Who's in Charge of Lincoln?, 527
Whose Town, 596
Wide Horizon, 494
Wild Angel, The, 1186
Wild on the Bases, 858
Wilderness Wedding, 1220
Wilderness Winter, 1219
Wildlife Cameraman, 727
Wind Blows Free, The, 493
Wind in the Rigging, 1043
Winds of March, The, 1303
Windy Foot at the County Fair, 552

TITLE INDEX

Wiser Than Winter, 1071
Witch World, 989
Witches' Sabbath, 351
With a Task Before Me, 455
With an Open Hand, 956
Wizard of Earthsea, The, 796
Wolves of Willoughby Chase, The, 9
Wonderful Flight to the Mushroom Planet, The, 237
Woodshed Mystery, The, 1288
Workhouse Child, The, 1208

Year of Enchantment, 1069
Yellow House Mystery, The, 1284
You Bet Your Boots, I Can, 686
Young Mark: The Story of a Venture, 33
Young Mustangers, The, 789
Young Unicorns, The, 802

Zero Stone, The, 977
Zip-Zip and His Flying Saucer, 1131
Zip-Zip and the Red Planet, 1133
Zip-Zip Goes to Venus, 1132